# MY LIFE WITH HORSES

# BY

# FILBY HOLDEN

My Life With Horses
by Filby Holden

ISBN No. 0-9695040-0-4

Publisher Filby Holden
Author Filby Holden

First Published Dec. 1990

Printed in Canada by The Beacon Herald Fine Printing Division

# MY LIFE WITH HORSES
## BY
## FILBY HOLDEN

*This book describes my own experiences and adventures of twenty years in the saddle, family life in the English Countryside, a holiday aboard the QE2 and adventures in Canada.*

*These chapters, some sad, some educational and many of them humorous, give a clear and vivid description of the scenery and portray many interesting characters and horses from the introduction to the final pages, and I would like to thank my family and friends for making it all possible.*

*FILBY HOLDEN*

# PROLOGUE.

During the war years, the lot of the teenager was not a happy one. The years of youth, spent in the services or beneath the ground in unwholesome air-raid shelters, left deep impressions in the minds of the lucky ones who survived.

These impressions from those unhappy times, they wanted to erase from their memory. When the boom time came, the time for those hardworking ones to play, play they did, in a very big way. To all those who recaptured their lost youth, who pursued and attained pleasure and unfulfilled ambitions, to absent friends and the ones we held dear and to the memories of a long gone era, I dedicate these chapters.

# INTRODUCTION.

I rested my arms on top of the old wooden gate and gazed across the meadow to the open fields beyond. The tears fell unchecked. A mist formed slowly before my eyes as memories from over the years came flooding back to me.

I could see in the distance the shapes of horses grazing as they stood head to tail to ward off the flies, swishing their tails in the summer's heat.

I saw the blackberry bushes, the green flowering hedges.

I remembered the wild yellow daffodils, that covered the fields every Spring.

The water trough, the row of stables, and the manure heap across the yard with its ever increasing load, piled high and steaming, waiting for someone to carry it away.

The wheelbarrow, the pitchfork leaning against the haystack, visions so real I could almost smell the hay.

I thought I heard the jingle of harness.

I saw the sunlight shining on the bits and bridles, smelled the polished saddles. My eyes strayed to where the hay-nets used to hang upon the stable wall.

The scene changed to Winter. Once more the horses appeared.

This time, even closer.

Puffs of steam rose high into the air from the horse's nostrils, as they munched on their breakfast from the buckets of oats and sugar beet.

I wanted to call out to them.

Frosty! Bridgit! Lady! Melody! Cobber!

But the shapes just faded away.

Many miles I had travelled across the Atlantic Ocean,

Just to visit the old haunts, once more.

# CONTENTS

PROLOGUE.
INTRODUCTION.
CHAPTER ONE            EARLY DAYS 1
CHAPTER TWO            FAMILY LIFE 7
CHAPTER THREE          ON THE MOVE 15
CHAPTER FOUR           THE ODD COLLECTION 23
CHAPTER FIVE           THE GREAT ESCAPE 31
CHAPTER SIX            THE POLICE HORSE 37
CHAPTER SEVEN          LADY JANE GREY 47
CHAPTER EIGHT          THE BIRTH OF A FOAL 55
CHAPTER NINE           RIDER IN FLIGHT 65
CHAPTER TEN            TO MATE A NANNY GOAT 79
CHAPTER ELEVEN         GYMKHANA TIME 89
CHAPTER TWELVE         OUR FARMER FRIENDS 95
CHAPTER THIRTEEN       A HORSE'S BRUSH WITH THE LAW 101
CHAPTER FOURTEEN       SAD TIDINGS 115
CHAPTER FIFTEEN        TWO TO GO A-HUNTING 123
CHAPTER SIXTEEN        FAREWELL TO A FRIEND 131
CHAPTER SEVENTEEN      WELCOME MELODY 141
CHAPTER EIGHTEEN       ANNIVERSARY ADVENTURES 147
CHAPTER NINETEEN       THE GYPSY 157
CHAPTER TWENTY         FROSTY 167
CHAPTER TWENTY-ONE     ACCIDENTS WILL HAPPEN 177
CHAPTER TWENTY-TWO     COACH AND PAIR 187
CHAPTER TWENTY-THREE   HORSEY HOLIDAY 193
CHAPTER TWENTY-FOUR    THE LAST GOOD-BYE'S 201
EPILOGUE.                        205

# Chapter One

# EARLY DAYS

Horses have always fascinated me. As a young girl I would reach up to stroke the milkman's pony. His name was Star, a handsome little grey who came sedately down the road each morning to deliver our two pints of milk. A smarter pony would have been hard to find. He knew which house to stop at and when to walk on. I'm sure he could have done the round on his own.

At the end of our road was the Co-op coal yard, and there every morning at the crack of dawn the big Clydesdale horses would be washed down, brushed and harnessed to the large coal wagons. There they would wait patiently for the sooty-black sacks of coal to be loaded, for delivery to the inhabitants of our neighbourhood.

Just about that time I was ready to set off for school, along would come Blackie with slow, ponderous strides, his head stretched forward, swaying from side to side. I always thought he was looking for me, as soon as they were close enough I would wave to catch the coal-man's eye. He would always stop and with a twinkle in his eye would shout.

"Hello Matey!" and to the horse, "whoa there old lad, your little mate's got something for ya!"

I would hold out my hand with two lumps of Tate and Lyle's finest sugar, and feel his soft rubbery lips mouth my palm.

I would obligingly wipe his chin dry with my clean handkerchief.

My exasperated mother often asked how I managed to get my handkerchief so messy and dirty every day. She must have also wondered how her sugar-lumps went so fast. I always kept the sugar well hidden within the deepest confines of my school satchel, along with my history, maths and spelling homework, and any other miscellaneous rubbish that I had collected during the week. Hands wandering among those hidden treasures were apt to come to a sticky end.

A few streets away were the other idols of my life, the big shire horses, that belonged to the Carter-Patterson goods carriers stables under the railway arches. The noise from the trains that passed overhead couldn't have worried the horses very much, as every time I visited them, they munched contentedly at their hay and never batted an eyelid. Even when we noisy kids trooped in to pay them a visit.

Most Saturday afternoons would find us city kids all out there; Billy and Doris Williams; Mr. and Mrs. Church's little brood, (there were eight of them); Dorothy White; the Barclay twins; Stan and Mary; and me, young Phil the tomboy. We took along anyone who could rob a family larder for a biscuit or an apple or two, then in a body we would descend upon the stable lads with our bribes, just to take a peek at the horses. More often than not, we tried to wheedle the lads to give us a quick trot around the stable yard.

I can hear our voices pleading even now, "Oh go on Mister, give us a ride please, you said you would if we were good and brought some sugar."

If we were lucky a chosen one of us would be hoisted up to sit upon a horse's bare back and be led around the stable yard.

"Hold tight to the mane," the stable lad would say. "Give a click click with your tongue, push into his ribs with your knees, give a little dig with your heels, and away you go."

The animal's flesh would be warm and wriggly to the touch and the skin seemed to ripple in little waves that made the shivers race up and down your spine. The warm steady breath coming out in snorts from the horse's nostrils appeared as steam rising from a kettle's spout. The smell of fresh hay in the manger was like nectar to our city lungs. We ignored the strong smell of ammonia coming up in whiffs from the horse's urine. Nothing could deter us from hanging around the stable yard as often as we could.

I was usually one of the lucky ones to get a ride, as my uncle Alfred was one of the stable lads. How I envied him then! How I wished that I, too, could work in a stable one day and have some of those magnificent creatures to look after. However, it was to be a very long time, before my wishes were finally to come true.

I was thirteen years old when my middle-aged parents and I moved away from the town to the countryside. I was a sickly child, and if there were any ailments going, sure enough I was the first to suffer. "Plenty of fresh air and sunshine that's what you want my girl," said my mother. "No more hanging around coal carts or mucky stables."

Poor old dear, didn't she think they had horses in the country? Was she in for a surprise; as she found out a few days later.

She had been busy putting the new house in order, arranging furniture and hanging curtains, so that the laundry day was delayed. However it had to be done and as the November day was quite dry with a strong wind blowing she decided to hang the laundry to dry outside. The trouble was there was no clothes pole onto which she could tie the clothes line to, only a large old oak tree at the end of the garden. Somehow or other, together, we did manage to fix the line to the tree and in no time at all a full line of laundry was blowing merrily in the breeze.

Being a busy woman and finding lots to do about the house, somehow or other the laundry was forgotten.

About six o'clock that evening mother suddenly remembered the laundry. "Oh dear!" she said, "I wonder if it's still on the line?"

She looked out of the back door at the now, pitch-black night. She shivered a little as the cold November air rushed to engulf her.

"Fetch me the linen basket," she said, "And the peg bag."

I hurried to do her bidding, but I never ventured beyond the door, I just stood in the open doorway, waiting.

"Come out and help me," she called, "I can't manage on my own it's so dark out here!"

We were groping our way along the clothes line when suddenly, mother stopped dead in her tracks. "Shush! Listen!" she said.

We both stood very still, straining our ears to listen, and to peer intently into the darkness.

"What's that?" mother whispered, "It sounds like heavy breathing and I'm sure someone is creeping along behind me."

"I can't hear anything," I whispered back.

We took a few more clothes off the line. "Shush! there it is again," she said, "and it's getting closer."

Suddenly, she gave a piercing scream, dropping the laundry in terror she ran towards the house, shouting out to me.

"Get inside quickly! There's something furry and black out there and it licked my face."

I shot past her, almost falling over the doorstep in my haste to escape the monster, or whatever it was that was lurking about in the inky darkness. Mother stumbled over me.

Once safely inside her trembling fingers reached up to the shelf to find some matches to light the oil lamp that she kept for emergencies. She placed the lamp on the back porch windowsill, its feeble light illuminating a small patch of the back garden. There was just enough light to see the prowling intruder.

It was a small, shaggy-maned, Welsh Pony, who being half blinded by the light in his face, gazed in astonishment at the two faces that were peering at him from the window. Probably wondering what all the fuss was about. When dad came home from work that evening, he was surprised to find mother still doing the laundry.

She explained, and told him of her terrifying ordeal, but his only comment was, "It was your idea to live in the country, you'll have to get used to it." However, the following Saturday afternoon, Dad was kept busy fencing the whole of the back yard, and no mention of horses, was ever made in my mother's presence again.

At that point in time a second-hand bicycle was my latest love and I became an ardent cyclist. With boys and girls of my own age we toured the surrounding countryside, going into the woods in Springtime and returning home late at night with tired legs, aching muscles, and clutching bunches of wilting bluebells. All that glorious summer of nineteen-thirty-nine, we went on picnics, and explored the backwaters of the River Thames. The boys made wooden rafts out of old discarded orange-crates, and the girls cut up old sheets and made them into sails. We paddled downstream looking for frogs and trying to fish. More than once it was my misfortune to fall into the river and I had to ride all the way home looking like a drowned rat.

I had reached the tender age of fourteen when the war started, evacuation was not for me. My parents said, "If we die, we all go together." The quiet war, it was called at first. Food rationing was our only bug-bear.

My father had served in the last war, so for our family, things went on pretty much as usual. But when the air-raids started there was no peace for anyone.

By nineteen forty-three, I joined the forces.

"You've got two arms! Two legs! and two Eyes!" said the medical officer. "You'll do!" She gave a loud yell, and I shot back startled. "Yes!" she said, "And you can hear quite well too."

I stuck with that outfit for three gruesome years, and it was during that time that I met my present husband. He was serving with the Canadian Forces Overseas, so in spite of war, life and love still go on no matter what happens to the cold old world outside.

Irene was our first post-war baby, plump, cuddly and very blonde. Two years after came Carl, our first son. A year and four months later Anthony was born. Two more sons came at three year intervals Laurence and Geoffrey. The other children for some reason or other found the name Geoffrey, hard to pronounce, so he was referred to as Netney.

The family grew like weeds and before we knew where we were some of them had turned into teenagers. There was a lapse of seven years, then as an afterthought, along came another son, Ray, and until he died he did bring a ray of sunshine into our lives and was thoroughly spoiled.

We were known to our friends as Phil and Bert, and the names stuck.

My husband, was affectionately known as BERTIE BASSETT, after the little man on the licorice box, the allsorts were the kids.

The children had so many friends between them that our house, although small, was always filled to overflowing. I often wondered, who were the guests and who were mine? Sometimes, it was hard work trying to get through the doorway. "Haven't you got any homes to go to?" I would yell, trying to be heard above the noise.

No room in the house was left unoccupied, not even the basement. Down there, Bertie, and the boys had their air-craft-modelling factory. As I opened the basement door, the smell of the glue they used, would drift up the stairs and make me sneeze and shudder.

"Go downstairs and clean up that mess," I would yell at them. I was a washing and cleaning fanatic — anything that stood still for too long, was either washed, or thrown away.

Our only spare time, such as it was, was taken up by the children's schooling projects; going to school plays and concerts at Christmas, attending children's parties, parents day, school fetes and sports days. Most were rather ordinary. I expected the summer sports day at Anthony's Technical College to be no exception.

I did want to go, but not with all the others in tow.

"Please say you'll come," Anthony pleaded, "all the other mothers will be there."

I considered thoughtfully. "I'll have to see if I can get your father to part up with some spending money first," I told him.

When I did ask Bertie, he fiddled about with the cups on the kitchen table. It was as if he expected to find some money hidden there. He pondered for a moment, then he said.

"How much do you want?"

I slowly replied. "Well! It will be two shillings entrance fee for me — and a shilling each, for all the kids."

I paused for a minute to let this sink in. I continued. "Then, they'll want ice-cream. Then there's the side-shows, and, some cold drinks."

His face went quite pale when he answered.

"What do you think my name is ... ROCKAFELLA!?"

So after an earnest discussion we agreed how much cheaper it would be if I only took Anthony.

"But what am I going to do with the others?" I asked him.

"Oh that's okay," he said. "You can leave them with me, I'll find them something to do in the store, and it won't cost me a penny!"

This was an offer I could hardly refuse, so before he changed his mind, I promised Anthony I would go. All I could think of was what a wonderfully quiet afternoon would be in store for me. But it was to be on this quiet afternoon that I was to make my re-acquaintance with horses....

# Chapter Two

# FAMILY LIFE

The great day dawned and with total misgiving I entrusted Carl and Laurence to Bertie's tender mercies. I left Geoffrey and Ray with a neighbour. Irene, went off with a friend for the day.

The rest of the morning I had a chance to prepare myself.

"What shall I wear?" I asked Anthony. He wasn't very helpful as he answered me with a noncommittal reply.

"Wear what you like, it's only a sports day and I can't see you taking part."

"It's going to be a very hot afternoon by the weather forecast," I told him, so I think I'll wear this cotton dress."

I shew him the garment to see if it met with his approval.

"That's okay," he said. "For goodness sake hurry up or it'll be over before we get there!"

The bus took us right to the school gates. We paid the spotty youth who was sitting by an upturned box by the entrance.

He gave us a grubby-looking ticket and pointed his finger in the direction of the playground.

"It's all going on in there," he said.

"There's a tent for the tea and some sideshows in the playing fields."

"Thanks," I said, as Anthony and I walked on to see what we could find to amuse us.

But Anthony, had ideas of his own, "Have you any money to spare for me?" he asked. Looking up at me his left eye squinting, his nose screwed up and his mouth puckered into a crafty grin.

I winked at him and nodded my head. "Here you are, here's five shillings, and don't tell the others how much I gave you."

"I won't say a word, honest, I promise," and he ran off to join his friends.

Left alone I scrutinized the sideshows that were set out in the playground. There was a hoop-la stall with cheap gaudy prizes set around in a haphazard fashion on a yellow and black checkered board, and on some of the squares stood prettily dressed dolls wearing very large hats that no amount of skillful throwing would allow a hoop to drop over. There were rectangular boxes, wrapped in bright shiny paper, also too big by far for a hoop to encircle.

I was just about to walk away when the smiling young lady who was in charge of the booth called out ...

"All you ring you get to take away; only two pence for three rings and every package contains a surprise."

"Certainly would be," I replied. "You would need a hula-hoop to get over that black cat."

"What black cat?" she said in surprise.

"Why, that one over there," I told her, pointing to a large, furry feline asleep in the corner.

"How did he get there?" she exclaimed. "Cheeky thing, shoo! shoo! Be off with you!" she cried as she gave the offending animal a tap with a long stick.

I did try my luck for a minute or two, but, unless the prize pushed itself under the hoop, I could see my chance of winning was nil.

A few feet away from the hoop-la stall, in a shady corner under a large sycamore tree, someone had placed half a dozen buckets on their sides in a row, their gaping tops opened like mouths awaiting their prey. On the far side of the buckets stood a cardboard box, it was full to the brim with tennis balls. I edged nearer.

"What do you have to do?" I asked, of a figure dressed as a clown who was obviously in charge.

"I'll show you," he said. "You aims the balls at the bucket, see, like this," With his right arm extended behind him and his hand clenched tightly over a tennis ball, he rocked back and forth on his heels several times, at the same time, he swung his arm like a pendulum on a grandfather clock. He finally let the ball go, and it flew through the air in the direction of the centre bucket, landed, and stayed put. He turned to me smiling.

"So," I said. I waited for him to go on.

"That's it," he said. "If the ball stays in the bucket you get a prize."

"Aren't you the sports master?" I asked him as I peered more closely into his face.

"Shush! Shush!" He whispered. "Don't tell anyone, I feel a right fool in this get-up."

"I'll keep quiet if you tell me what the prize is," I answered him in the same quiet tone. He looked around carefully to see if anyone was within earshot, then he leaned forward and with a suppressed chuckle, he said, "It's a PIG....."

"That's something I could very well do without," I told him. "I have enough feeding problems at home."

Our conversation and laughter had attracted some customers, and I could see that he would be very busy for the rest of the afternoon. How he would come up with enough pigs, if there were too many prize winners, I shuddered to think as I wandered off to explore the rest of the stands.

The darts booth was more to my liking. Seeing a likely customer the tall red-headed young man in white flannel trousers and cream coloured shirt, left his post by the row of dilapidated dart-boards and made his way over towards me. "Come on, try your luck," he said. "Three darts for a shilling, if you hit the ace or king you get your money back; hit three high cards and you get a goldfish."

Biting on my fingernail for a moment in deep concentration as my eyes moved from the dart board to the tank of swimming fish I thought, why not!, it looked easy enough and I had thrown a few darts in my time. Then I thought about the shilling and changed my mind. "No!" I said to myself, I'd better not. Knowing me I would probably hit that nice young man instead, and I didn't fancy carrying a goldfish around for the rest of the afternoon, anyway.

The sky, which had been clear and bright blue for the better part of the day, now started to cloud over and a few drops of rain began to fall. I sought shelter in the refreshment tent. I made my way over to the counter, picked up a tray and joined the line of people waiting to be served. Then I sat for awhile sipping my drink and munching away on a biscuit and looking around. Suddenly I spotted Anthony who was sitting with some friends. There was something tied to the leg of his table. No! It couldn't be. I reached into my purse for my spectacles and hastily put them on.

I almost dropped them in my astonishment, for there under the table and busily eating a sticky bun, was a fat, little piglet.

"Oh no!" I gasped, as I knocked the chair over in my haste to get to the table where the boys were sitting; and to find out to whom that piglet belonged.

I should have guessed before I asked. Four faces looked up at me wreathed in smiles, all anxious to tell me the good news.

"Look what Anthony's won!" they cho, rused together. I didn't know what to say, words failed me for once. All I could picture was the bus conductor's face as we tried to board his bus, with a pig in tow on a piece of string. Would he charge full, or half fare for his unique passenger? "You had best telephone your father," I said to Anthony, "And have him drive us home." The other boys thought it was all a huge joke, but, when I told them they could look after it until six o'clock, that didn't please them at all.

The rain had stopped and the sun was out once again.

It was nice to have some time to myself and a place to escape to even if it was only for a few hours. The crowd seemed thickest by the second-hand bookstall so I set off in that direction to hide myself amongst the book lovers. I loved to browse through old books whenever I had the chance, but before I had gone a few yards I was stopped by two small schoolgirls.

"Hello! Where's the fire Mrs. Holden?" they said. My mind had been so preoccupied that I had failed to see, or recognize the girls. They were the Stacey twins and they lived in the next street to me. The taller of the two, Mary, was carrying a large iced cake on a silver tray, and her sister Elizabeth, held a thick wad of small pieces of blank paper in her hand.

"We're selling tickets for the Guess-the-weight-of-the-cake contest." said Mary. "Would you like to buy some?"

"Sure!" I said. "I'll have a couple of tries." I had no idea what the cake would weigh, I only knew that if I had made it, it would have weighed a ton.

The Co-op's Christmas cakes at our local store tipped the scales at roughly six pounds. I wrote that down. And just to be on the safe side, on the other piece of paper, I wrote down five pounds-four ounces. "Hope you win the cake, Mrs. Holden," shouted the girls. "So do I," I replied. "If we can't eat it all, the pig can have what's left," I could hear them laughing as they walked away.

I continued to roam around the sideshows until my feet ached but I never won a darn thing, so I decided to seek pastures new.

I walked through the school gates and out into the playing field where I slipped off my shoes to tread the velvety carpet of springy turf. The smell of the damp earth made moist by that afternoon's shower intoxicated me somewhat, and I was overcome with a sudden passionate urge to dance, as there wasn't a soul in sight. However, I overcame this as I could see there was something going on in the far end of the field. I could hear the noise from a crowd of boisterous spectators who were jumping up and down flapping their arms, appearing to me as a line of linen blowing dry on a wintry day. I could hear shouts of, "Come on old chap you can do it. Come on! Come on! The blues."

There were others shouting. "Come on! Come on! The Yellow's. Oh no! The red's are winning now." I realized it was the school house-team-race, that was taking place. I was just about to join the throng of spectators to see if Anthony was taking part, when another sound reached out to me.

Did my ears deceive me? Was it a horse's whinny that I heard? The sound seemed to be coming from my left, so I turned sharply, and followed my nose in that direction. A vision began to take shape. There before my eyes in a roped-off paddock stood a large, but docile-looking horse. I walked across to the paddock to get a closer look, when a voice that startled me called out.

"Good Afternoon! Beautiful day, isn't it?" I looked about me in surprise. A tall, slim girl in her early teens came out from behind a stack of straw and made her way towards me, she came over to the makeshift gate in slow easy strides, resting her arms on the top rail. She appeared to be a friendly type. So I said to her....

"He's gorgeous, isn't he?"

I could see he was a gelding of maybe fifteen hands, a bright chestnut cob, with a thick muscled neck. "I bet he's strong," I remarked.

"Yes he is," she said. "What's his name?" I asked, "And how old is he?"

She must have thought I was extremely nosey. However, she did seem willing to talk about him.

"He is just five," she said. "And his name is Rocky and he is quite gentle really in spite of his size."

"Are you giving rides on him?" I asked her.

"Yes," she said. 'Why don't you round off your day with a nice quiet ride?"......

"I'd love to!" I smiled as I said this, just to hide my nervousness.

"But it's been a long time since I sat a horse, I feel a little scared now; suppose I come off?"

I was dying to have a ride really but the thought of hurting myself made me hesitate.

"Come on! It'll be okay," she assured me. "Don't be nervous, I'll hold on to him for awhile. He's so good, honestly, he wouldn't hurt a fly,"

"I'm not really dressed for it," I said, still hesitant and doing my best to back off, without losing face.

"He'll only walk-on slowly, and there's nobody to see your knees here," she giggled.

"Oh all right then, you've talked me into it," I giggled nervously back.

"Come on Rocky!" she spoke softly to the Cob as she untied the gate and led him out into the open field.

"Be kind to this nice lady," she said, "and give her a pleasant ride."

"Do you know how to mount a horse?" she asked. I nodded my head knowingly, "Sure," I said.

But as I stood close up to the animal's left side to take hold of the reins and to place my left foot in the stirrup, the Cob, suddenly seemed to have grown a mile high.

Now during the course of our conversation, the young owner had been so busy praising her horse's virtues, that she had forgotten to tighten the saddle's girth, and as I put my whole weight in the stirrup to mount, the saddle slipped around the horse's belly and my anatomy ... went with it...

The poor beast took umbridge at this unseemly behaviour. With a loud snort and a mighty buck, he kicked up his heels and dashed off full pelt around the perimeter of the field, with me still clutching the reins and hanging almost upside down. With one foot up his flank and the other under his belly, we charged round and round. With me screaming like a marauding Indian warrior attacking a wagon train.

No! I never fell off, sheer fright must have glued me to that saddle. It was a miracle I never broke my neck.

When he finally outran himself and skidded to a halt, he was sweating and lathered in foam, the strong odour of leather filled the air. I slid to the ground in a daze. Shocked faces peered at me as I tried to stand upright, my knees had turned to jelly and I was sure I was going to faint.

Someone's arms were around me trying to give me support. Someone else, held a cup of cool water to my lips.

I just couldn't stop shaking.

The fields and the horse were still there — but where had all the people sprung from?

Regaining my composure at last, a sudden thought struck me, I could feel my face getting hotter and hotter as I realized, what parts of myself and my underwear ... must have been showing in that mad dash around the field.

I was pondering on this, when I felt a frantic tugging at my dress. For one awful moment I thought it was the horse, coming after me to take his revenge.

But no! It was my son Anthony, he looked very cross, as he said to me ....

"Mother! You shew me up in front of all my school friends, screaming like that! And showing all your underwear."

He didn't seem to care about my feelings at all.

"Oh," I said. "I wonder what you would have done in that position, laughed?"

I resolved there and then, that, Never! Never! Never! Would I ever get up onto a horse's back again.

I suppose we have all made that kind of promise to ourselves sometime or other. Never to do it again.

# Chapter Three

# ON THE MOVE

The years passed all too quickly it was time to move on. Our small house seemed to be shrinking as the children grew into adults. There simply wasn't enough room for four full grown lads and their larger bicycles, or for two working teenagers who constantly fought for the bathroom each morning, or for my husband and our eldest son who made frantic efforts to reach the bathroom shaving socket first, as soon as dear daughter vacated the bathroom with her bag of makeup. So, we decided the most practical thing to do was to move to a larger house.

My husband had recently made the acquaintance of a master builder, during his coffee break at a nearby cafe; a Mr. Brian, who, being a family man, understood the situation perfectly and offered to help. A few weeks later this charming fresh-faced Irishman called on us, his hands full of plans, blue prints, and glossy photographs and a list of house-prices.

The latter, Bertie scrutinized very carefully.

"Now!" said Mr. Brian, "I've got the very thing for you Bert. There's a nice little plot of land in the countryside and not too far away from your store. As a matter of fact I shall be starting to build within the next few weeks. That's if you're interested? Come along to the office next Saturday. Bring the wife!"

The following Saturday afternoon, not only me, but the whole family with Mr. Brian leading the way trooped down to the proposed site.

It was a quiet rural village some three miles from the nearest town. There were no paved roads to speak of; and the place had an air of desolation. The freshly-dug earth was damp beneath my feet and a cold raw wind swept across from the surrounding fields. On each side of the narrow main highway which faced the site, were two Olde Worlde Inns, The Shepherd and The Swan.

The latter of the two stood well back from the road, and, in front of the gravelled-forecourt, was a large duck pond. The grassy banks around it were uneven and sloping, and the lane, which continued in each direction from the forecourt, was no more than a dirt and cinder track, which,

I was to discover later merged into the Ongar Road, where it turned and twisted and wound snake-fashion through the countryside, until it reached the tiny village of Ongar in one direction, and the busy town of Brentwood, in the other.

This busy highway would hold many exciting moments for me in the years to come.

There were only a dozen houses being built at that time, the spot planned for ours was to be at the very end of the road. At the right hand side of the plot was a small pasture, then a wooded area which ran alongside the Swan Inn's gardens, then gradually extended to the rear of our property, to link up with roughly eighteen acres of grazing land. A ditch and hedges separated the paddock and gardens from the main fields. There were no fences or gates that I could see, but what did catch my eye was the pleasing sight of two small ponies that were tied and grazing under a tree.

Irene and I suddenly lost all interest in the why's and wherefore's of house structure, drainage and other worldly problems. All we were interested in were the ponies and the scenery.

There was no sign of the younger boys, last seen they were heading in the direction of the pond. However, they did come back eventually, wet, and extremely grubby. They told me they had found a small island, some tall trees and masses of conkers.

"When are we moving Dad?" they asked, when we joined the others. "We can't wait to climb those trees."

"It looks like you've been climbing them already," I said, as I noticed their dirty knees. Was I doing the right thing? I wondered.

When I said, "I'll think about it," I suppose the ponies and the scenic layout depicted in the glossy brochure did help me make up my mind, so, there was no quibbling or arguments when we were asked by Mr. Brian.... "Would you like a house here?"

However, it was to be towards the end of November nineteen-sixty-three before the house was ready to move into.

Now all new houses have a certain amount of dust, paper, and odd pieces of rubbish left behind by the builders; and this house was no exception. Sometimes cleaning ladies are employed to clear away the mess, but, being anxious to move in quickly, we chose to do the cleaning ourselves. The two older boys offered to help. So armed with mops, brooms and brushes, buckets and dusters, we set off one cold dark evening to do the necessary chores. This turned out to be an adventure that we hadn't bargained for!

Bertie had purchased a new light van some weeks previously and this was to be its first long-distance trip, so naturally, we proceeded with the utmost caution over the unfamiliar terrain. There were no street lights in this part of the country which made for even further caution. We thought we were almost there, when, from out of the misty darkness there appeared a lone cyclist, riding along at a snail's pace.

"What's wrong," I asked Bertie, as we slowed down.

"Nothing's wrong, but do you want me to run the poor man over? Perhaps he's lost too," Bertie replied.

I turned to my husband to make a sarcastic remark, and as I did so I noticed that the steering wheel he was clutching was well away from its moorings, I looked at him in astonishment.

Not being a driver or having any mechanical knowledge at all, I said to him, "Put that steering wheel back! What do you think you're playing at?" He laughed in a peculiar way.

"You B... fool," he said. "I can't! the dam thing's broken off!"

"There's no need to swear in front of the boys," I said.

"But what are we going to do now?"

"Get out and push it I suppose," he said crossly. "What do you think I should do? Pray!"

He got out of the van and walked around to the back to let the boys out, I walked behind grumbling, the two boys helped their father hand-steer those wheels half a mile to the new house.

There it remained until we moved in, the first part of our belongings to be installed. How to get home? That was the question on all our minds.

"Well, now we're here, we might as well do what we came to do," I said. "There must be a bus service into the nearest town, we can find out about later." "I noticed a pub along the road," said Anthony. "Perhaps after we've cleaned the house we can go there for some potato-chips and lemonade and ask them if we can use their phone to call a taxi."

"Good idea," I replied. "Let's do that."

Problem settled we set to work with renewed vigour. We must have resembled a trio of tramps when we were through.

"Time to clean up ourselves now!" I said. It was then that I realized that although we had taken the tools to clean the house, we had forgotten to take a brush or even a comb to make ourselves look respectable. Well, not for a moment did we imagine that we would be paying a call on the local pub, and in such a scruffy state too. However, it couldn't be helped, so we locked the house door and set off for the tavern to the grey-stoned building, a one-time haunt of Jack Shepherd the highwayman. It was well set back from the road and to gain access to this hostelry one had to cross a sharp-stoned court-yard, the only illumination being a solitary lamp fixed to a high pole.

Under the lamp and swinging in the wind on creaking hinges was the Inn's sign. It was hard to read in the poor light, but after peering up at it intently, Carl said, "It's The Shepherd! Shall we go inside? It's jolly cold out here!"

We made our way across the courtyard towards a dim light that came from a partially covered window. Its eerie glow cast weird shadows upon the green entrance door, which squeaked and groaned as I pushed it open to step cautiously inside.

The others followed me in!

It was like walking in upon a scene from a play by Charles Dickens. A long wooden counter with a raised flap occupied most of the oak-paneled room, and the flag-stoned floor was covered by a sprinkling of fine sawdust. From the oak-beamed ceiling hung two ship's lanterns which gave forth a pale insipid light. To the left of the room was a large open fireplace and in the hearth a fire burned with a warm and cheerful glow; its flames cast flickering shadows to dance from wall to ceiling leaving the cavernous corners in semi-darkness. The only furniture to be seen were a few hard wooden benches and three dark-stained trestle tables, but at the side of the fireplace was an old wooden settle. The seat was covered with a cloth of dark crimson velvet fastened down with small brass studs that winked and sparkled in the firelight. As did the old-fashioned brass warming pan, the pewter mugs, and several horse-brasses that held pride of place upon the mantle shelf.

All this I was fascinated by whilst my husband explained our predicament to the solitary figure behind the bar.

I heard my husband say!

"Is it okay if we bring the boys in? It's so cold outside."

The landlord smiled at the boys, as he came out from behind the bar. The lads who by this time had stepped out from behind me were gazing in open-mouth wonder at what they thought; as they told me later, was a scene from the past. Then, the landlord, a small white-haired gentleman in his later years came over to us almost bowing in an old-fashioned way.

"Good evening," he said "What a cold dreary night it is to be sure, you must be half frozen, sit yourselves down by the fire: that's right! make yourselves comfortable. I don't think anyone will mind the boys being in here — when I explain."

"Your husband's been telling me what happened to your van, it must have been a terrible shock. Good thing you were off the highway, and a good thing old Fred here," (He pointed to a country yokel who was sipping ale in the far corner of the bar) — "Was riding his bicycle so slowly, otherwise, you may have ended up in the Swan's duck pond across the way."

He chuckled; But I didn't think it was very funny.

Fred nodded and waved to us from his side of the bar, Bertie, beckoned him over and asked him to have a drink, Fred accepted and came over to join us. It seemed that Fred, knew all about the local transport, buses and the like, and all the local gossip too. The general layout of the countryside he knew by heart, and he had a young family. "Two boys about your ages," he told the lads. "They'll show you around."

While all this useful information was being stored in our minds, the landlord it seemed, had retired to an inner sanctum. He returned a little later with a plate of sandwiches, some cocoa for the boys: and a drink for Bertie and I. Whilst we were enjoying this homely fare a young couple came into the Inn, ordered drinks, then, came over to join us by the fireside. Fred, being a friendly type seemed to take great delight in relating to them our evening's mishap. Thank goodness he did! For as it transpired, this couple were to be our new neighbours; and after hearing of our misfortune; and as they knew the area where we were living already; they offered to take us home. We never did get around to telling them just how many children we had; we didn't want to spoil their first impressions. Little did they know what was to be in store for them in the next few years ... living next to a large family ... and that, was before the horses ...

However, I shall never forget the first Christmas in our new home, looking out onto the unfamiliar sights of green fields, countless trees, and hearing the constant mooing of cows as they grazed in the pasture just a field away. Listening to the village church bells of St. Nichols at the end of Church Lane.

The tranquility of the surrounding countryside was awe-inspiring.

Since moving we hadn't had very much time to make new friends as November had been a busy month for us all.

We knew Sally and John of course from our previous meeting, but, we had yet to meet the family who occupied the house on their far side.

We never had long to wait, for on Christmas morning I was awakened by the sound of excited voices, they were coming from the direction of the field that lay at the bottom of our garden. And, as my bedroom was at the back of the house I could hear them quite plainly. I could contain my curiosity no longer, I had to get out of bed and go across to the window; collecting my spectacles on the way.

A welcoming sight met my eyes! For there in the field, stood a small group of people, they were gathered around a small boy who sat astride a midget-sized Welsh Pony.

I was so excited that I never bothered to wake the rest of the family as I dressed hurriedly and went downstairs.

I had to see the pony up close, whatever those people thought of me, I just didn't care.

I donned a coat and an old pair of Wellington boots and slipped out of the back door treading gingerly across the muddy garden to where that chattering bunch of people stood.

"Hello!" I said. Flashing them all my biggest smile.

"Is this pony your present from Santa sonny?" I asked the dark-haired boy. The rest of his family stood back; to give me a clearer view of the boy and his mount.

The lad's dark eyes lit up and he gave me a winning smile as he nodded his head in answer to my question.

The proud parents, then introduced themselves and we were soon on first name terms and chatting away like old friends.

They had only moved into their house a week before Christmas, although as Vic and his wife June explained to me, they were actually local people.

They had just fancied a new house, one with some open land behind it; somewhere to keep ponies and maybe a few horses.

My ears pricked up instantly!

These people, I must make friends with ....

I hadn't forgotten my last experience on a horse, NO! Not by a long shot; but there was no harm in just looking at them!

Later that evening we asked our new neighbours in for a drink to celebrate the festive season, they accepted; and brought along their daughter Susan, their son Michael, and June's brother. We discovered we all shared the same interests.

Horses! The love of the open air and the countryside.

It wasn't very long after this meeting that Vic, persuaded Bertie to buy our first pony.

His name was FROSTY! an unbroken gelding of two years. A dark bay, with a black mane and tail, four white socks and a white blaze, starting from his soft warm brown eyes, to the tip of his be-whiskered nose.

He looked so docile — as if butter wouldn't melt in his mouth.

He stood fourteen-hands high, and, as we found out later, he was full of the fiery spirit of The New Forest Pony.

He wasn't very expensive and a second-hand bridle and saddle were thrown in the deal for good measure.

THEN THE FUN BEGAN .....

# Chapter Four

# THE ODD COLLECTION

I was a greenhorn ... and so was my daughter, as far as horses were concerned. My husband did have some knowledge of work-horses from time spent on his father's farm, before the war years. But this pony, was something else.

He really was wild and full of himself and not at all keen on having a rider on his back, or having a strong bit in his mouth, and just putting the saddle on him was a feat in itself.

So after Irene had cracked a few ribs and rendered a few unmentionable places black and blue, the Pony was pronounced "BROKEN-IN" ..... Bert, thought Frosty was then safe enough for other members of the family to ride.

Surprise! Surprise! I volunteered to ride him first. In those days I didn't weigh very much and as Frosty was a stockily built pony, I thought we made a fine pair.

From my newly acquired horsey friends, I purchased the necessary equipment of what I thought that the best-dressed rider should wear. A hard hat, to protect my head, long black leather riding-boots to encase my legs, and a rather large pair of riding breeches, from my oldest lad I borrowed a white shirt and a black tie. In this get-up I was to be found riding the range in Vic's rented fields almost every Thursday afternoon.

My fond spouse would stand by the gate (with eyes partly closed at times) and his heart in his mouth.

However, in spite of the jeers from my lads and unkind comments, I made rapid progress and was eventually let out of the gate to savour the delights of the scenery of the open road.

A few months later we were coaxed into buying another pony, this mount was for my youngest son Ray who by then was four years old. The pony's name was Tiny ... he stood twelve-hands high and ran as fast as the wind, so we renamed him, "Speedy Gonzales."

On several occasions when I made my way back to the fields from an afternoon's ride, I noticed an elfin-faced little girl of about eight years hang-

ing about by the top field gate, so one afternoon I reined in to speak to her.
"Hello!" I said. "What's your name?"
"It's Shirley!" She said.
"Are you looking for the horses?" I asked her.
"Yes" she said, "I come here every day after school, I love horses."
She went on to tell me that she had just had her eighth birthday and how disappointed she had been at not receiving her most treasured wish. I had a good idea as to what it was, by the way she looked wistfully up at Frosty.
"I go to riding lessons," she informed me, "I can ride quite well."
I looked into her eager face, her bright, blue eyes were shining, and her long chestnut, shoulder-length hair hung in soft curls about her shoulders. She chatted on, I listened carefully. Then a sudden thought occurred to me about Speedy, I thought how nice it would be if this little girl could encourage Ray to ride. Maybe she could help take care of the pony too, then she could exercise him as part of her reward.
I asked her where she lived and if I could meet her parents, I thought I should ask their permission first before putting the idea to the child; it would avoid any disappointment later, should they refuse. As it transpired I met the mother at the post office, and Shirley was with her. The child must have explained who I was and how we met. The mother smiled in my direction, I smiled back as I went over to speak with her.
"Is it okay for Shirley to come over and ride our pony sometimes?" I asked. "And would you mind very much if she helped to feed and groom him?" I explained my plan for her daughter to teach Ray to ride and of the reward I had in mind.
"Would you also allow Shirley to go riding with my daughter, or myself, sometimes, we would take great care of her."
The mother agreed, then she said. "As long as she does her homework first, and she doesn't get in your way, that's fine by me."
This brief encounter, was to be the start of a wonderful friendship, between Shirley, her family and ourselves. It was to last for many years. From that moment on until Shirley reached her early thirties, she was my inspiration, my constant riding companion, help-mate and friend; as my older sons were never really interested in riding, just when it suited them, or if they wanted to show off in front of their girl friends.
So, it was either Irene and Shirley, or Shirley and I that did most of the riding, and when the girls were too busy I would take Ray out riding with me, with Speedy on a lead rein.

This arrangement was fine for a time, but we thought it would be much nicer, if us three girls, could all go out together, as we now had too many riders and not enough mounts.

On my twenty-fifth wedding anniversary; and after a good many falls and tumbles and double-somersaults over horse's heads; the family declared me brave enough to have a larger mount of my own. My anniversary gift from them, was a shiny, black-coated mare. An Irish Hunter, sporting a white blaze on her face, four white socks and large gentle eyes. She stood fifteen-hands high, and nearly as wide ... I did wonder at the time if the family had tried very hard to find me a mare with the widest berth possible to affix my posterior to, to make sure I stayed in the saddle. Anyway, every time I mounted her I felt like I was doing the acrobatic splits.

Our local blacksmith from whom the family had bought her, had called her "JET", inappropriate for a lady, so I changed her name to "BRIDGIT" which sounded more Irish to me.

The blacksmith said she was gentle, and wouldn't hurt a fly, but what he never told me was, that she'd had very little experience out on the highway; and had never been in heavy traffic. This I found out soon enough, when I encountered double-decker buses, which scared her half to death. The mere sound of chimes from the ice-cream van, or the ringing of church bells would send her careering down the road at break-neck speed.

More than once she took to flight when encountering these situations in narrow country lanes, especially at harvest time, when the heavy farm-tractors and machinery were abroad. If it hadn't been for Shirley and Frosty, I don't know where we would have ended up, head first in a ditch I shouldn't wonder.

But in all our years of wanderings together not once did she purposely unseat me. Maybe, someone was watching over me. Maybe I was just dead lucky ... not everyone else was, as she did her level best to try to unseat everyone else who tried to ride her, especially in the show-jumping ring. Show-jumping — she hated.

I never tried it with her, the only jumping she enjoyed was when we rode through the forest, or, out hunting.

Towards the end of August, Shirley, and Allen, her dad, with Irene in tow, went to look at a Cob that was owned by our local milkman and was up for sale. His name was Cobber, a sturdy, rough-haired chestnut pony of about fourteen-two. His coat appeared almost ginger in colour in the strong sunlight; and his mane and tail were a fiery red. He had been in harness for some time so he was sound in wind and limb; and very reliable in traffic and easy to shoe and box.

Everyone agreed, he was an excellent choice for Shirley, and that same evening Allan bought him for her, and she rode him home, where he was formally introduced to the rest of her family, and after a gift of carrots from Shirley's mum; he joined Frosty, Bridgit, and Speedy in the eight acre fields, and after the first kick or two they settled down well together.

Cobber was soon to be the boss however, staying close to his harem of equine ladies; and protecting Speedy whenever he thought his food bucket was threatened by the other two.

All through the late Autumn, some of the finer days of winter and into the early Spring, found the three of us, Phil, Shirley and Irene, now known as the Three Musketeers ... riding out for miles. Mind you, I had to work longer hours in the evenings doing my household chores, so that I could explore the open road during the daylight hours.

Now keeping horses wasn't all fun and games, there were plenty of other chores to do besides riding. The horses had to be groomed before being tacked-up, which took a great deal of my time and energy, not to mention patience.

Then I would lose patience, especially if after all that performance down would come the rain. Although sometimes it never deterred me I would still go riding and get extremely wet. Or, I would get mad — pack everying into the car and go home, but whatever happened, after every ride the horses still had to be fed and watered, the water trough filled and the stables cleaned out.

There was always some kind of chore to do.

I was already general exerciser, mucker-out of stables, nurse, (More of that later). Blanket and bandage washer, saddle and tack cleaner and bucket scrubber, not to mention helping out with the harvesting of hay and fence mending ... all hard graft and unpaid of course. However, I thought it all worth while, especially when I remember the pranks that Shirley and I used to get up to.

Like the time she dared me to do a circus trick by standing up on Bridgit's back and trotting around the field real fast just holding the reins in one hand. And the day she made me jump over a wide ditch which seemed a mile across.

"You jump," she said, "Or I'll jolly well leave you there."

And as it was getting dark — I did. The fun we had when scrumping for apples from on high in the saddle. Only to find, that after all the trouble we had gone to, to get them, the apples were so sour that even the horses refused to eat them, and for all my efforts all I did was to swallow a fly which made me cough and splutter for the next half mile.

Summer evenings and Sunday afternoons we would hack for miles stopping at country Inns for a ham or cheese roll with a soft drink to wash it down, although sometimes I could have done with something a little stronger to vanquish the frights.

My swift panicky gallops on Bridgit, occasioned by heavy transport, back-firing trucks, a line of wind-whipped laundry, soon made my name a byword in that small village. I was known as the Mad-capped Rider of Kelvedon Hatch.

Meantime, the business of keeping horses had so excited my spouse that he took it unto himself to purchase a thoroughbred Mare, (Lady Jane Grey), in order to enter the world of show-jumping.

I was not to take part in this venture, (perish the thought), just Shirley and Diane, another young rider that we had recently met. If I were to hurt myself, who would have done the chores or looked after the animals if they were sick?

I did experience some amusing episodes when doing this.

There was the time when Frosty, managed to cut his leg.

The first thing I did was to send for the vet. He came post haste, that's how caring he was. After he had treated the wound, he asked me if I had had very much experience dealing with this kind of wound..

"You know you must keep it as clean as possible," he said.

Well I thought, any fool knows that, but appearing as I thought knowledgeable I replied.

"I suppose I will have to think of something, that will not only keep it clean, but stay in place at the same time?"

"It won't be easy," he said, "But I'm sure you'll think of something."

It was to be later that evening whilst ironing the boys clothes that I came upon a pair of knee-holed pyjamas.

My mind worked overtime. There's a good idea, I thought, containing my mirth as I conjured up a picture of Frosty, with his wound attired in a knee-length, blue-striped, pyjama leg.

However it did work; and for a week or so Frosty, could be seen strutting proudly around the paddock in his colourful bandage which was tied from his foreleg up to his neck then up and over his head by a red leg bandage, to where it sported a bow, just above one ear. This every day performance of his attracted an audience of the village children who were kind enough to give him special treats as they gazed at him in wonder from the other side of the fence.

Then there was the time that Frosty, was very, very, sick, when he caught the dreaded fever called strangles.

Now Frosty was like me in some ways if there were any complaints going around he was sure to get them. So, when he started to cough like mad I sent at once for the vet.

The vet and I were quite used to each other by now, I think he had a little more faith in my capabilities as a horse's nurse..

"This is going to be a real task for you," he said.

"I hope you can run fast?" he laughed. I wondered why.

I was to find out why — soon enough, as he went on to explain the treatment.

"I want you to make up a poultice bag with this powder I'm going to give you to put on Frosty's neck. Be sure to change it every half hour. It must be kept hot. I'm also going to leave you these pills. You must make sure he swallows them!"

"Hold his jaws open wide and drop one down his throat, whatever you do, don't let him spit them out."

He motioned with his hands as to how I should carry out his instructions. I looked at him in amazement, picturing, in my mind what would happen if by some unlucky chance he swallowed one of those large pills. I thanked the vet profusely, but after he had taken his leave I got to thinking ....

Now the stables were a good hundred yards away from the house, so, in order to keep the poultice piping hot I would have to do a very fast sprint indeed, so, every half hour, on the dot, saw me, charging across the field to the stable; with a bucket of hot water in one hand, (or what was left of it after I'd slopped it everywhere) and the wrapped up dressing in the other. Thus, I managed to keep the poor creatures temperature down, but was I ever tired by the end of the first day. The pill episode was yet to come.

I got Frosty's mouth open okay, but his eyes rolled up in fright and he backed away from me in panic as I endeavoured to push my arm halfway down his windpipe. His head shot up and the pill shot down his throat, but after he'd swallowed it his jaws clamped down on the sleeve of my best sheepskin coat, my arm, still inside it.

I gave him a dig in the ribs in panic, open came his mouth, and my sleeved arm and hand emerged, they were covered by a wet, sticky, slimy substance — and, large teeth marks.

By this time I was getting used to pain inflicted on me by horses, especially when fastening the girth on a saddle. Bridgit, was the worst offender. She had this nasty habit of blowing out her belly whenever this had to be done.

More often that not, the prongs on the buckle would slip and go right down my thumbnail, and sometimes she would step back and plonk her hefty, great, hoof on my foot; and the harder I tried to retrieve it, the harder she would lean on it and press down.

That's why I never wore the rubber boots, after her hoof on one's toe they wouldn't have lasted very long.

But it was all very painful.

There was so much to learn about these handsome creatures, and I had only just begun, but, I was to learn fast; and, I would get to see much more of the veterinary than I ever saw of my own family doctor.

# Chapter Five

# THE GREAT ESCAPE

As I said before, horses are hard to catch in an open field especially when you have work for them to do, and they are harder to catch when they escape from their enclosure, such as, when trespassers break down fences or leave gates open.

Then the police would be hot-foot on their trail, the horses that is, the trespassers usually got off scot-free.

Our village policeman swore by polo-peppermints for catching runaways, and he should know, by previous experience.

The Essex Constabulary.... were the only officers I knew that carried peppermints, ropes and halters in their cruisers.

Now horses are like people in some respects.

The grass is always greener on the other side, so I was not surprised when one miserable wet morning, the phone rang!.

"Mrs. Holden," said a voice in authoritative tones.

"Yes, speaking," I replied.

The grave-toned voice continued.

"This is the Brentwood Police."

"Yes!" I said, I had a feeling what he was going to say next.

"I think some of your horses are out and wandering about on the Blackmoor Road."

"I'm very sorry," I said, "But are you sure they're mine?"

The voice of the constable then proceeded to give me a detailed description of the wrong-doers.

"Yes, it sounds like mine," I said.

"I'll get them in as soon as possible, I'm very sorry," I said once again, "But it will take me some time to walk up there and I will have to get someone to help me first."

"That's okay," the voice replied.

"I'll bring someone to help you and we'll run you down there. We have your address."

Within ten minutes and before I had managed to assemble the necessary catching tackle, the police car was at my door.

I gave the tack to the driver and he stowed it away in the back of the car.

"Get in the back," the officer said to me. I did as he bid and we drove slowly along the street and as we did so I noticed several curious neighbours trying to peer into the window.

On reaching the main road we drove very slowly hoping to spot the wanderers, however they were nowhere to be seen.

"I think I'll look into the fields before we go any further, they may have finished their sortie and gone back there."

Sure enough there they were meandering among the flowerbeds in the gardens of Blackmore House. At least two of them were, Frosty and Bridgit, Lady...one of the new thoroughbreds had managed to work her way into one of the enclosed tennis-courts. How?, was certainly a puzzle to me, as she stood sixteen hands and the gate of the court's enclosure was only five foot high, and not very wide.

I went back to the two policemen who were propping-up the gate. "They're in here," I shouted.

I just had two halters with a piece of rope attached to them with me, but the policemen never had a rope of any kind.

The horses, still sampling the forbidden fruit of the garden were in no hurry to be taken away, but after a brief struggle I did get Frosty haltered and led away, and everywhere he went, Bridgit was sure to follow, so I had no problems with her. Those two I reinstated with a worried Cobber, who by that time was frantically rushing back and forth along the other side of the fence. Once Frosty and Bridgit were back in their rightful place I decided to search for the escape route first before seeing to Lady. I found it at last, it was in the top field adjacent to the garden. It seemed that a large old Elm tree that the gardener had been sawing down had somehow fallen in the wrong direction, and landed on the wire fence crushing it down flat leaving a gap big enough for the horses to step over.

I found some old fence post and string and fixed it up for the time being. I would see to it later as soon as Lady was in.

In the meantime, I had asked one of the officers to shut the gate leading into the tennis courts, I hoped he had! I wanted to make sure that Lady, would remain a prisoner of her own making. I also sincerely hoped that no one from the big house would want to play tennis that morning. Perhaps the rain was a blessing in disguise.

It had been raining rather heavily all that week and the fields were extremely muddy as only grazing fields can be after a very wet summer.

My boots had become very slippery and were caked in mud especially after my reconnoitre of the fields.

Fence mended, now was the time to sort out Lady. She must have sensed that the other horses were missing, when I went back to her she was prancing up and down in extreme agitation inside the small enclosure. I didn't think I could manage to extradite her by myself, so I went back to the boys in blue who were still leaning on the gate and in earnest conversation with the gardener.

This instigator of my troubles yelled out the minute he spotted me.

"You'll have to get that blasted animal out of my tennis courts as soon as you can, do you hear me?"

"I will! I will!" I yelled back at him, "That's if those two gentlemen you're gabbing to can spare me their valuable time."

"I'm not too keen on horses," said one of the so called helpers as he turned away. The other policeman however seeing my crestfallen face, took pity on me.

"Come on Mrs. I'll help you," he said.

He took off his peaked cap and gave it to his friend.

"I think I'll manage better without this on," he said.

I wished later, that he had taken his jacket off too.

We approached the gate with caution, I gave my help-mate some peppermints and told him to wait outside.

"I'll go in first," I said. "And I'll try to coax her out."

"If she dashes past me, then you can try to catch her." "You've got some string, or something, haven't you?" I asked him. He shook his head.

"Oh dear! that's too bad," I told him, "I only have one halter left."

"Perhaps you could use your belt," I said.

"I don't think that will be long enough," he replied.

"It would be if I tie my raincoat belt to it," I said.

"That should make it long enough."

He removed his belt from his trousers and I tied the two belts together and handed them back to him.

Then hiding the improvised halter behind his back, as I had directed, he took his stance outside the tennis court gate.

I opened the gate warily and stood quietly inside for a minute or two, then I walked slowly forward towards the Mare, stopping on my way to pluck a handful of clovered-grass.

Her head turned towards me as she saw me coming, and her ears went right back, a sure sign of aggression.

I thought, this is it, I bet it isn't going to be easy.

I spoke softly to her as I held out my hand with the peace offering, she advanced with caution sniffing at the grass in my hand, her mouth opened over my palm.

"Got Yer!" I said.

Seizing my opportunity I held on to her nose with my free hand and with the other hand I made ready to put on the halter.

But the Mare, had ideas of her own.

Firstly, she gave a leap sideways, then she spun around and tried to deliver a hefty kick in my direction, she missed, then, with her head bent low she made a dash for the open gate and freedom ...

However, once outside the gate she stopped dead in her tracks.

Did she sense that the long arm of the law was outside waiting to capture her?

But what really did surprise me — was that the law — was ready to take so swift an action.

With a loud whoop of triumph the waiting officer threw the make-shift halter over lady's head where it slipped down around her neck and held fast.

But what that poor man didn't bargain for — was, that as Lady leapt up, he slipped, and landed face downward in the mud his beltless trousers going down, down, with him, impeding his every move.

The mare took off ...

Why that brave man never let go, I often wondered, grim determination I shouldn't wonder made him hold on fast.

He was pulled — well, half dragged across the muddy field for a good few yards, with me chasing after them brandishing the other halter and trying to keep up.

Eventually, Lady stopped and I managed to get the halter on her and give the very embarrassed and cross policeman his trouser-belt back.

Of the other police officer, there was no sign.

At least, not until we had reached the top gate near the main highway, to where he stood quietly puffing away on a cigarette.

He should never have laughed so much when he saw us, I thought his compatriot was going to knock his head off, or worse.

Mission completed the officers took me home.

I did offer them some tea, I also offered my brave hero the loan of some dry clothes.

Both officers, flatly refused.

Then I was silly enough to suggest that perhaps, I could teach my kind helper to ride.

When he growled the words.

"NO THANKS!"

I wasn't at all surprised.

I only hoped and prayed, that if those horses ever escaped again, he wouldn't be the one to respond to the call.

I guessed he would have felt the same way too.

So, later that year I kind of trembled in my shoes when I answered the phone and another policeman was on the line.

REQUESTING — TO SPEAK TO — ME ..........

# Chapter Six

# THE POLICE HORSE

"Hello! can I speak to Mrs. Holden?"

"Speaking," I said.

The man's voice on the other end of the line came over loud and clear. "This is the Brentwood Police," he said.

I gripped the receiver tightly, I never replied for a moment, my mind was ticking away as to what I thought he might be going to say next. When I finally spoke I could hardly recognize my own voice as it had risen to a rather peculiar squeaky pitch. Gathering up my courage I asked, "Are the horses out again?"

I thought I might as well take the bull by the horns and find out straight away.

"No, nothing like that," he said.

I sighed with relief.

"I have a friend," he went on, "he owns a retired police horse. Now he's going away on a month's holiday soon and he wondered if you would be prepared to look after it while he's away. Take it out for exercise and so on."

"Can you tell me a little about the horse?" I asked him.

"Well," he replied. "He's a gelding, sixteen hands, well mannered, and, being an ex-police horse, naturally he's very safe in traffic. "Mr. Banks, my friend," he continued, "will tell you more about him, that's if you're interested, and he also said if you do decide to look after his gelding, will you please let him know as soon as possible. I'll give you his phone number now."

"Thank you," I said, "but I shall have to ask my husband first, you can tell Mr. Banks I'll phone him later."

"Okay," the officer replied, "I'll see he gets the message." And with that last remark he put the phone down.

That evening Bertie and I discussed the possibility of entertaining a new boarder, and we agreed to take him in.

I was quite excited at the prospect of riding a well-trained, road-worthy animal for a change, so I contacted the owner that same evening. He seemed delighted by our decision and said he would bring Major, his horse, over the following Sunday morning for a formal introduction.

Sunday morning found me up bright and early, ready to receive my two guests, but before the streets were aired, or I had eaten any breakfast, I heard the familiar clip-clop, clip-clop sounds of a horse coming down the road.

I dashed to the window as was customary for me when hearing that magnetic sound, and there, coming down the road towards my house, I saw them. "The Horse" and his rider, so this was Major.

He was a magnificent creature of sixteen-hands and as white as the driven snow, I remembered hoping his habits would match his colouring. He had a thick neck and a proud head which he held high; he was slimmer than Bridgit, but with a longer back and heavier hind-quarters, denoting strength. His silken mane and well-brushed tail conveyed to all that he was always well-groomed.

Astride his highly-polished saddle sat a fresh-faced young man, leaning slightly forward as he rode, his head bent as his inquiring eyes seemed to be seeking out the house numbers.

As he drew closer I called out to him. "Here I am, over here, you are Mr. Banks I presume?"

"Ah! Good morning," he exclaimed, as I walked to the end of the path to meet him. "Fine day! Isn't it?"

Was it? I hadn't seen much of it yet; my eyes were too full of this dream — of a horse.

I knew I was going to enjoy exercising him without having a worry about traffic. Frosty was in training for show-jumping about this time, so Shirley was exercising him, leaving me a little more free time to ride another horse, besides Bridgit.

While I was busy thinking about all this, the cheerful stranger had alighted from his steed and was handing me Major's bridle. We shook hands as I turned to him and said.

"Would you like to follow me, I'll take you over to the stables. We can get the horse settled in first, then go over to the house to talk."

"Very nice," remarked Major's owner when we arrived at the vacant stable.

The white gelding looked around him as if studying his new surroundings, and as I entered the stable to see the horse in, I purposely banged the door and rattled the bolt a few times to see what his reactions to sudden noise would be.

I don't know why I bothered, because he never so much as flickered an eyelash. Instead, he focused his undivided attention on the mare in the facing stable, or was it Lady's full net of hay swaying to and fro that was fascinating him?

We left Major to explore his new abode, and to make the acquaintance of his stable mate from across the cobblestone path.

Mr. Banks and I also made sure that the horse was left with a full bucket of water and a net of fresh hay before we finally left him, then I invited his owner to come back to the house to discuss the price of his geldings board and lodging over a cup of tea; and by the time we got back to the house the rest of the family were up and about all clamouring to see the new arrival.

"Now you'll just have to wait until after breakfast," I told them.

"I'm just about to make this gentleman a cup of tea."

Over the tea cups I explained to Mr. Banks that we rented the stables from the Landlord of the Swan Inn, and I told him how hard we had all worked to get them into tip-top shape after so many years of disuse and neglect.

"We are allowed full use of the paddock too." I told him.

"We exercise the horses there, and the girls who ride for us train Frosty and Lady there, for show-jumping. We also keep two horses and a pony in the fields behind Blackmore House, the grazing land, we share with our neighbour."

"You were very lucky to find so much grazing land," he said.

"Yes." I said, "and all the land behind Blackmore House, right through to Outings Lane, we actually rent from a farmer friend from Roxwell; you see it's not suitable for farming crops anyway and the horses help to keep the grass down."

Mr. Banks having finished his tea and our business concluded, bade us all good-bye. He said he was going to his vegetable plot to give it a last minute tidy.

"I really must see to it," he said, "before I embark on my holiday."

He departed joyfully, pleased in the thought no doubt that his trusty steed would be left in capable hands.

The next morning was pleasantly warm and once my chores had been completed I thought it would be a good time to take Major out for a hack. So, with his bridle over my shoulder and his saddle over one arm and a bag full of assorted brushes over the other I set out for the stables.

Major greeted me with a loud whinny.!

"Hello old lad," I said. "Want to come out for an airing?" He put his head over the door and nudged me and as I drew the bolt on the stable door I offered him a polo peppermint; just to be on the safe side, giving him a gentle push so I could get by. Then sorting out the brushes and comb I started to groom him. He was a perfect gentleman to tack-up and saddle and he almost stood to attention as I prepared to mount.

So far, so good I thought. Once mounted we were ready to set off.

He trotted out across the paddock until we reached the gate, there, I dismounted to lead him through; making sure I closed the gate behind me. Across the garden we went, then out into the road where I remounted. Then with the command of "Walk on Major," we started out for the highway for what I thought was going to be a nice quiet hack .....

Feeling somewhat over confident I began to relax a little to enjoy the ride and admire the scenery.

It was a beautiful morning in early August and the sun shone brightly from a cloudless blue sky.

I left the road to walk through the small pathway that led into Swan Lane, and as I did so, I heard the draymen singing as they rattled the bottles and banged the crates whilst making their beer delivery to The Swan Inn. They looked over when they saw me and gave a cheery wave, I waved back. Then putting Major into a trot I rode across the grass area by Swan pond, being very careful to skirt the immaculate lawns of Fox Hatch House. The village home for the elderly. Here, some of the seniors were reclining in lawn chairs enjoying the fine weather. They too waved, as I trotted by.

Now I had to cross the road, but before I could go, some feathered creatures had decided to do likewise.

They crossed in front of Major's hooves, not a bit scared, as they waited in single file at the kerb side until the road was clear. Then Mrs. Duck, and her seven siblings with beaks stretched forward to their limits waddled slowly across the road to the Shepherd Inn's pond, for their early morning dip.

They were seemingly unaware of the comic picture they made, and I thought what a nerve they had, to reside at the Swan Inn, and to drink their fill at The Shepherd.

When they were safely across we followed in their wake.

Passing The Shepherd Inn, I guided my mount to the right and we continued on our way along the Blackmore Road to the woods, where the Blackmore Road finished and the Ongar to Brentwood Road resumed.

*Phil on Major*

We passed the small coppice of Birch, Beach and Larchwood trees, their Autumn leaves turning from green to gold's and brown's. We passed the bus stop where a few people stood waiting for the Green-Line Bus to Brentwood.

Looking across to my right I could see the fields and meadows of Brizes Park. The stately home of the Hon. Simon Rodney, Squire and country gentleman, who every year kindly gave the villagers his permission to use the fields on his estate for their annual gymkhana.

The next hundred yards or so I decided that this portion of the road was not safe for sightseeing or dawdling as it was one of the busiest sections in that area. Buses, trucks, cars and vehicles of all kinds were fast-moving here, and the paved-path on either side was also very narrow. Even a skillful rider with a traffic-proof horse had their work cut out to keep calm on this stretch of the highway.

However, once past the row of tiny, stone-built cottages, (built in the seventeen hundreds) and whose miniature gardens almost came in contact with the passing traffic, the road widened.

While the traffic was still in possession of most of the road a side strip of grass land was made available on the left side for nature lovers, dog walkers and horse riders.

I was sure of the two former uses, but of the latter I had my doubts, but we did make full use of it anyway, it was some respite from the motorists.

There was a high privet hedge which ran alongside this grassland that served a duel purpose.

One, to hide the early morning golfers on the Bently Golf course from the envious eyes of the hard working truck drivers; and two, to stop any stray golf balls from knocking-off the hats of passing horse riders.

At the shout of ...."Fore".... One was always inclined to duck.

Getting thus far, it was almost 12:30 when I passed the golf course and reined-in, turned off from the main road to pass the village school's playing fields where some of the children were playing, after their lunch break.

However, the few lads that I next encountered must have been home for their lunch and were just on their way back to school when I met them. They also must have been feeling very brave or they were full of mischief: why they were carrying long sticks was beyond my comprehension.

Whatever the reason, they brandished the long pieces of wood right in front of Major's nose in what might be described as a menacing fashion. I was nervous.... wondering what Major's reactions would be, but there was no need; with nostrils twitching and a fearful snort he leapt forward and without harming the boys he cornered them up against the school wall. You should have seen the expressions on those lads faces ... Talk about scared, I'd take a bet on it, they would never try a stunt of that nature again.

After a few Yells! Of "Mind my feet Horsey," and, "Will he bite Missus?" I decided they had learned their lesson. I proceeded to deliver them a stern lecture on how to behave around horses.

Lecture delivered, I rode on.

I thought I'd try a short cut to go home, through the opening in the hedge, I rode then alongside the Ashwell's Drive side of the golf course and out again into Days Lane along the wide grass verges, here I challenged my warrior mount.

"What about a brisk trot along here," I asked him.

His Breer! Breer! of an answer came soon enough.

So taking it as an assent of approval I gathered up his reins as a signal to trot-on. Then a strange thing happened!

The gelding sprang to attention before following out my command.

I was so astounded that I slipped sideways in the saddle and almost fell off. Much later I found out why he did this, or so his owner surmised.

"Probably, all to do with his extensive training I shouldn't wonder," said Mr. Banks. "Is that why he has a military name do you think?" I asked. Then I explained to Mr. Banks about a Major I knew when I served in the forces. "He used to stand to attention." I said. "Every time he spoke to you."

Mr. Banks just smiled.

But to go on with the story.

We came to the part of the lane that was very picturesque, narrow and winding. There were a few cottages on one side with rather long gardens full of brightly coloured flowers and masses of fruit and vegetables, and some of the owners actually kept goats, and one old man who I had often seen tending his garden and who lived in the end cottage, kept donkeys, and there were usually two of them tethered beside his front gate. I always gave this cottage a wide berth when out riding on Frosty, "Donkeys" he hated. I think the vibrant sound of the Hee Haw! Hee Hawing! Upset him.

Now luckily enough — although right out in the sticks so to speak some of these cottages did possess a telephone, and the connecting poles for these phones along this particular lane were spaced roughly twenty-five yards apart, and one of these poles was to figure in the next amusing episode.

Amusing to everyone, that is, except the luckless young man who Major spotted up aloft this pole, and who appeared to be in some difficulty, as the belt that supported his work trousers had broken, so with both hands fully occupied with the tools of his trade there was little he could do to remedy the situation. Thus we came upon him in his hour of need.

His trousers at half-mast! Well down below his knees; and to add a splash of colour to the scene, he was displaying a nifty pair of bright-blue underpants. And the light breeze that I had enjoyed on that warm August afternoon had suddenly changed into a sharp wind played havoc with his shirt tail billowing out behind him, reminding me of a ship in full sail, only needing a flag to top it all off. I was almost tempted to salute him, but I resisted and called up to him instead.

"Ship Ahoy! Are you in trouble?"

"Looks bloody well like it, don't it?" he yelled down. "Don't just stand there and gape, see if you can get some help."

Apart from laughing, which didn't amuse the pole-percher very much, I didn't think there was much I could do and I didn't think Major could help in any way. I'd never seen a horse climb a pole yet. The man on high addressed me once more.

"You're not much use to me." he said, "or your silly "BBB" of a nag. Go and get a ladder or something, I've got to get down from here before some other silly fools gather."

"Okay," I said, "Keep your shirt on, I'll ride up the lane and see if I can find someone with a ladder."

Meanwhile, Major seemed reluctant to leave, he seemed fascinated, his eyes transfixed; he was probably wondering what all the fuss was about; I had to tap him with the riding crop before he would turn away.

I rode back the way we came to the nearest cottage that possessed a telephone. I alighted from the saddle looping Major's reins around the fence post and dashed up the garden path to the cottage door, praying that somebody would be home.

It was the home of the donkey lover. It seemed like ages before someone responded to my pounding on the door, then he never opened it, not at first. I was just about to go when a side window opened and a scowling face topped by an old black cap, poked it's head out of the window.

It was the little old man himself.

"What do you want, what's all the noise about.?"

"Go away! Go away!" he said, "Can't a poor old man get any sleep around here? If you're selling anything, I don't want it."

"Go away! Go away!."

I walked over to the window to reason with this grumpy, old man.

"That's right! That's right! Stamp all over my plants you damn fool. Can't you look where you're treading?" he yelled.

"I'm sorry." I said, although I didn't feel like it, "But can you come to the door? I can explain."

"Explain what?" he said "You've done the damage now."

"There's someone in trouble." I told him. "We need your help."

Now whether this made him feel important, I don't know, but his head disappeared from the window and within a few seconds he was at the door.

"Why didn't you say so in the first place," he said, when I told him what I wanted. "Yes," he said, "You can use the phone, come in, and while you're talking, I'll fetch 'me ladder." Once he fully understood he complied helpfully. It took some time however as the old man was slightly deaf. I did try using lip-reading techniques and gestures to communicate, I think the old fellah's first thoughts were, that it was my underwear that was slipping. I shouldn't have been at all surprised if he had handed me a packet of safety pins. Or perhaps my interpretation of the catastrophe was somewhat vague.

I telephoned the company and explained to them the troubles of their luckless engineer — they said they would get on to it straightaway. By this time however, the now willing helper had found his ladder, some twine, and a large packet of old-fashioned safety pins.

While I rode on in front, he followed on behind, as fast as his short, bandy legs would carry him. By the time we reached the engineer, who must have felt quite chilly by then — a small crowd had gathered at the base of the pole — some offering up some ludicrous suggestions. However, there was one bright person who had the presence of mind to fetch a padded cover.

"Hi Mister!" she cried, "Throw your tools down on to this cover, you can hoist your pants up then." It was probably the only sensible suggestion that he had heard all afternoon.

He threw his tools down, one by one. Meantime, the old man who had brought an extremely short ladder which would only reach halfway up the pole, proceeded to climb it, steadily upwards. When he had reached as far as it would go he clumsily tried to throw up some twine, but as his hand let go of the ladder it swayed drunkenly and the old man fought frantically to retain his balance; but to no avail. With an oath and a loud yell, he slithered gracefully down. The crowd, gasped in alarm, then cheered, as the rescuing hero seemed to be unhurt.

Anyway, the engineer did somehow manage to fix up his pants and climb down the pole using his irons.

There was more cheering, much to his embarrassment.

He turned to thank me then came over to stroke Major's nose and apologize for his unkind remarks about us.

"Think nothing of it," I said, "But if I were you, I'd wear two belts from now on — and a pair of braces, before aspiring to such great heights."

Seeing there was nothing more that I could do, and as it was fast approaching suppertime, and I hoped to reach the stables before my hungry family came home, I hurried on.

The younger boys would be home from school by four-thirty, but I did have a good excuse for being late this day, and, I would have a funny story to relate to them for the after-supper entertainment. But the other horses had to be fed first and Shirley my help-mate would soon be around to fill up the food buckets; and I was just busting to tell her of my afternoon's exploits.

# Chapter Seven

# LADY JANE GREY

Now I did mention earlier about my spouse's interest in show jumping and the Mare that he bought, LADY JANE GREY the XIII. And now I would like to take this opportunity to tell you a little more about her and her introduction to the fold.

What an aristocratic title I thought, well bred she might have been, but she was also very stubborn.

You've heard the old saying, "You can take a horse to water, but you can't make it drink." Never a truer word was spoken.

Little did we realize on that fine March morning when we saw the notice in the paper, what we were letting ourselves in for.

The advertisement read:

SHOW-JUMPER....MARE....PART ARAB....FIFTEEN HANDS
QUIET TO SHOE....BOX....AND GROOM
CALL AFTER 6 P.M.

and there listed below was a local telephone number.

Irene, sharp of eye where horse news was concerned quickly spotted this announcement and that very evening put a call through to the Mare's home.

It was a shame that the Mare never answered the call herself to tell us in her own words what she was really like, what a difference that might have made.

However, the owners agreed to let Irene try the mare out and they set a time for her to visit. The following Friday evening Irene, accompanied by her father went to Crow Green Lane to see this illustrious animal.

Irene rode her around the stable yard. "She seemed fine," she told me later. "And I fell in love with her at first sight."

She sang her praises so much, that Bertie said he would buy her. So, when I returned from feeding the horses I was informed that we had another mouth to feed.

More buckets to clean! And fill!. More mucking out! More manure! Would it never end?

Some folks were excited at this new addition to the fold.

The stable behind the Swan Inn was set to rights, transformed! Fit for royalty it seemed. Well, not royalty exactly; just the Tudor-name equestrian beauty who was to grace our stables.

When I complained about how much she had cost, Irene said she would buy her, herself.

On the Sunday morning, Irene was driven to the Crow Green stables by Bertie himself. "More money than sense," I retorted as they set off.

The stables were in the small village of Coxtie Green, a very pretty part of Essex. The long, winding lanes that twisted and turned were beset by tall trees and privet hedges.

There was also a bridle path that ran through the woods that made riding a pleasure, especially in Springtime; when bluebells and primroses covered the soft earth, and no other forms of transport marred its tranquility.

No doubt these pleasures to come were in the forefront of the rider's mind as she set forth that morning.

Was she in for a big surprise .....

When they arrived at the stables, the mare, who had been groomed and well-brushed — stood patiently waiting to be tacked-up.

This was soon accomplished, and rider and mare were ready to set off for the mare's new home. That was the general idea!

But, it was not to be ....

Bridle on! Bit in mouth! Saddle in place!, that part went off without a hitch. The mare seemed eager to be off, and going out of the stable yard, was plain sailing. Even to the first half-mile the couple hit it off splendidly. But alas! there the co-operation ended.

Maybe, Lady Jane had taken a distinct dislike to the rider? Maybe the saddle sat too high? Or maybe the bit, wasn't to her liking? Who knows! Perhaps she hadn't been fed? That makes any horse mad — to be ridden out without its oats. Anyway, what I heard later was ....

That she reared up and pranced about on her back legs, tossing her head from side to side, she bucked and turned around and around in circles; making Irene feel dizzy.

"She tried her best to get me off," Irene told me.

"Probably wanted to get back to where she came from," I said.

Before Irene set out, my husband had left the stables to drive on ahead. He said he stopped the car about a mile along the lane to wait until the horse and rider put in appearance.

He waited and waited for some time, then he began to get a little worried as no sign of the couple was to be seen. So he turned around and went back a few yards and waited in a farm gateway. His imagination running riot so much that he could stand the suspense no longer.

He drove back the way he had come to see what had become of the wanderers. By now, he was sure there was something wrong.

Sure enough, there they were, around the next bend in the lane. There seemed to be an argument taking place.

The rider had dismounted and was shaking the whip in a threatening manner to the un-mounted terror whose snorts and twitchings suggested that, she was going no place without putting up a struggle. Taking stock of the situation, Bertie decided that this was no safe spot for further consultations with the unwilling animal, at least, not traffic-wise. So, after a brief discussion, car driver took over from the un-seated rider.

The new rider, Bertie, was a strong, heavyset man, and just as stubborn as the mare. My husband had taken command, fine! But who was to drive the car home? They were very lucky in that respect, as a friend who was riding a bicycle just happened to be in the vicinity. Fate?, could very well have been.

So, that Sunday morning saw, one sportily-dressed cyclist turned motorist, the motorist, un-booted and spurless turned horseman and a well-turned-out disillusioned rider, hiding in the back seat of a car.

Now whether Lady, (as she was aptly named on show-less days), preferred to be ridden by a member of the opposite sex or no, remained to be seen, but there were no further mishaps for the rest of the journey.

This argumentative attitude was to remain with her until she met her match, in a young lady rider named Diane.

Diane, was a brilliant horsewoman, she could encourage a horse to jump in any show ring, with or without a saddle.

In fact, when I watched her practicing in the bottom field with her long black hair streaming out behind her in the wind, she reminded me of a North American Indian, from a Western film: as she crouched low and forward over the horse's neck to jump bare-backed over the highest fences, then clear the ditch and gallop away into the distance.

There was only one mare that would never jump for her, or anyone else for that matter, and that was BRIDGIT......

I must say that Lady, settled down quite nicely once she had been fed and watered and for a time she occupied a stall next to Frosty, and they went through their paces together in the adjoining paddock.

Several girls had the pleasure of riding her in the show-ring where she performed with grace and skill, she also won many trophies in the showing and jumping classes.

One local show that I vividly recall took place at the Norton Heath Riding School, which was situated some eight miles from my home.

There was no one else free that day to hack Lady to the show, so I offered my services; I also promised to look after her until Diane, was free to take her into the ring.

Ever brave was I! No thought of what could befall me!

So, on a fine morning in early September I set off.

I was really looking forward to the ride, and as I went over to the stables to groom and tack Lady up and lead her out onto the road I hummed a few bars of "EMPTY SADDLES". Talk about tempting fate. We reached Swan Lane, turned right, and at the very end of the lane we rode into the woods and then trotted through the bridle path that ran parallel to the village green.

Through the gaps between the trees I could see a crowd of lads kicking a football around, practicing for the afternoon's match no doubt. I never stopped to watch but carried on along the leafy well-trodden path that would bring us out to the middle of School Road. But before we reached the road however, we would have to pass the large house on the hill .... and there lived the dreaded MONSTER .... Well, that's what I called him.

How else would you describe a fiend who terrorized country walkers and riders alike. This large canine creature, full of fury, would lie in wait for the unsuspecting traveller behind a high fence that separated his territory from the woods. Then, as his victim drew near he would rise up in a frenzy, leaping and jumping with all the force he could muster, to heave his whole body at the fence. He snarled, showing fearsome fangs as he ran up and down like a caged lion ..... barking his head off.

This day was no exception, he was there, there was no escape! He proceeded to do his usual terrorist act, barking like mad and leaping higher than ever.

He was wasting his time, the noise, however fearful did not deter her Ladyship. She never faltered, but with her head held regally high she walked on.

There was little traffic on the highway as we ventured forth onto the Blackmore Road. The hay had been harvested, so I knew there was little chance that we would encounter any tractors or formidable farm-machinery.

The mare walked-out well, she looked sleek and trim as her tail and mane glistened in the sunlight, a silky sheen of grey flecked with gold. Her coat of fine hair was of such a pale grey as to appear almost white when seen from a distance.

She was spirited and fiery and needed no riding crop to help her on her way.

I noticed quite a difference riding this mare, especially after riding Bridgit. Lady's shape was completely different. Whereas Bridgit, was a heavy mare with a long broad back, and well-covered withers; Lady's withers were high and rather bony. Bridgit, walked out with a heavier, firmer tread, Lady's light mincing steps were more like a prancer; and of course, Lady, was much more reliable in traffic.

I was itching to trot out, but trotting on the hard surface of the road was a No! No! This kind of practice could well result in the animal contacting splints and ruining their legs. Although I had often seen other riders do this.

Bertie, should have been behind them — they would have been in for a real long lecture.

Further along the road some horse-boxes passed me by, but all I could see was the rump end of the passengers — very hard to recognize them from that end. The drivers seemed to be in a hurry, but I wasn't.

The mare was still in good form and stepping out well and I was having a great time.

The events in which we had entered Lady would not be taking place until around noon and I didn't want to rush the mare and get her all sweated-up or excited; and besides, there was so much to see on such a fine morning.

Someone had started a new roof of thatch on the centre cottage near old Mr. Bill's Barn, and the owner of the next farm was busily painting his barn doors, and as I passed the farmhouse I noticed they had some pretty new yellow curtains hanging at the top windows. There was a long line of washing blowing in the breeze in the garden of the end cottage; and way pass the cottages at the beginning of the next row of hedges I could see quite a few ripe blackberries, some were small yet, but they would soon be black, large and juicy. I made a mental note of this for future pickings.

The thought of juice and wanting something to drink made me push Lady on a little, promising myself a drink as soon as I reached my destination.

Eventually we reached the stable yard of the riding school establishment. I knew most of the girls who worked there and the riding master, Mr. Colby (more of him later) and I nodded and smiled to them as they returned my salutations. I noticed the admiring glances that they were bestowing on my mount; and it made me feel proud to be seen seated astride such a good looking mare.

Some of the girls walked over to comment on Lady, as they asked the usual questions. Such as.

"What's her name?"

"How old is she?"

"Where did you get her?" "What events are you entering her for?" I answered all their questions with some witty remarks, about where she would be placed if I tried to jump her. They laughed knowing full well that I never did any show-jumping.

I left the girls as I rode on, out through the paddock to the outer fields beyond; to where the rings were roped off for the various events, my eyes searching anxiously for Diane. I was hoping to pass Lady over to her so that I could be free to go in search of some light refreshment, and maybe mingle with some of my friends who had promised to be there.

I had to trot around the field twice before I found my co-rider, she was busily chatting to a group of dismounted riders, I noticed she had a paper cup in her hand, so she had managed to get herself a drink. I pulled Lady up sharply and trotted over to where she stood.

"Hi Diane!" I said.

"Oh you got here!" Was her only answer.

Then she turned tail and walked away to join her comrades.

"Hi! Where do you think you're going?" I asked her. "I thought, once I got here, you were going to take over, or did I imagine it was here that Lady and I were to part company?"

How wrong I was!

True, Diane did take her into the ring on several occasions and they did win some ribbons during the course of the day. The rest of the time, which was to be twelve hours — I had that mare, to stand by, to brush and water and to be her general nursemaid.

From eight o'clock that morning until eight o'clock that night, tired, hot and dusty, that was me, and I wished all shows and horses to blazes ....

By six o'clock I'd had enough, so, without bidding anyone adieu I mounted up and with a few other weary, saddle-sore colleagues we hit the trail and headed out for home pastures.

We rode out two abreast. There was Jane, her sister Tina, Sylvia, and myself; and some others I can't recall.

Strange to tell, the horses were still lively, and with their heads held high they walked smartly on, some displaying their rosettes of blue, red, green and yellow silks, tied in fashion to the cheekstraps of their bridles.

A brisk walk took us about two miles from the stables of Norton Heath, to the first empty stretch of stubble field about half a mile in length.

Now the girls in the front of the column had remarked that it would soon be dark, and they were anxious to get off the road.

However I don't quite recall whose idea it was to go into that field for a half-mile gallop; but I decided it certainly wasn't going to be me!.

But, at the first opening gap in the hedge the others dashed into the field and were away like crazy, galloping full pelt up to the end gate.

Before I had a chance to say "Yea!" or "Neigh!" .... Lady took off, with the bit between her teeth and her neck stretched to the fullest she dashed up the road in full pursuit.

Now when a horse takes it into its head to bolt off with you, it's no use sawing on the bit; not unless you want to come off backwards; and if they perchance to buck, you could very well experience that mad flight over their head. I usually found (after three successive flights in that manner) the best way to keep your seat, was to sit well-down in the saddle; and to keep your feet firmly in the stirrups, your toes should be pointed up and your heels firmly down.

Thinking on those lines, although it was with some difficulty I did retain my seat I peered intently as I flashed by looking for a gap in the hedge. But the mare had other ideas!

She, could jump the hedge ... and she, was going to prove it! with — or without me.

We cleared the hedge — together ... to the other side; and wonder upon wonder — I was still up there.

True, I was still astride the mare — but in the saddle? no way ... I was positioned around her neck.

My booted feet covering her eyes! and my riding cap, almost covering mine — and the reins — dingle-dangling!

We continued in this fashion to the end of the field to where the rest of the riders were calmly waiting.

"That was jolly good," Tina said. "I never knew you could jump?"

"Neither did I," I breathlessly replied.

I never let them hear the few choice words that I muttered into Lady's ear as I straightened up to resume the journey — or to tell them how scared I had been, so I was really glad when we came to the fork in the road and we had to part company. I bade them all farewell and continued the rest of the journey in silence — and alone.

When I finally arrived back at the Doddinghurst fields to turn Lady out to graze, I saw my husband waiting by the open gate.

"Where the devil have you been?" he said, as he gave me a searching look and came closer. I thought he was going to smell my breath, in case I had stopped for a quick drink on the way back, I wish I had done so.

"Do you realize what time it is?" he went on. "You — should know better than to tire your mount out like this. She's all sweated up! Get off!"

The last request of his was easier said than done. My legs were fixed to a position akin to a Bronco Buster, I was sure I would be bandy for life.

"And happy trails to you," I said, as he helped me down from the saddle. "Any more moaning and you can take her to the rest of the shows yourself!"

I was saddle-sore, weary and really mad.

"It was your idea to take her," he said, as he stroked and fussed over Lady.

"I know it was," I replied. "But, I didn't think I would be out on her all that time; and doing most of the looking after too. Diane, only had her for the eventing," I told him, with an injured air of a martyr.

"Anyway, you're back now," Bertie said. "So stop beefing and help me load the buckets and tack."

We drove home in silence, except for Bertie's last cheeky remark.

"I'll go back and feed Lady later and give her a check over! You — can get your own tea! — can't you?"

By his last remark I was beginning to wonder — who was the most important — Lady — or me? ....

I never told him what had happened in the field, probably someone else would tell him later. I, was too tired to care.

When I had time to think of some of the crazy things I did do, it was no wonder that later in life I was to have both of my hips replaced; which was to end my riding days — forever.

# Chapter Eight

# THE BIRTH OF A FOAL

Now although I never competed in any of the show-jumping events, I did enjoy entering in the Gymkhana's.

Shirley and I would usually hack to the show-grounds together.

Irene never took part, but she did enjoy getting the horses ready and helping the organizers, as willing hands were always welcomed. There were so many jobs to do, before and after the actual events took place.

There were the show-rings to be roped off, numbered cards to be given out to the competitors, microphones and loud hailers to fix up, show jumps to be erected, and water to be laid on for the four-legged competitors, and a refreshment tent to be set up for the spectators and the riders.

Not forgetting the "THUNDER BOXES" .... A term used for the outside Ladies and Gents .....

Most of the jobs had been done the night before, the finishing touches were added very early the next morning, and everyone who had worked so hard to make it all happen, would say.

"Please God .... Don't let it rain."

On these special days, which were usually Saturdays, Irene would be up at the crack of dawn, and after swallowing down a cup of coffee she would arm herself with a bucket and brushes and take herself off to the stables, to where the horses that were to take part had been ridden up the previous evening.

Once there, Irene would devote her time to the beautification of the competitors in question.

Lady, for the showing, Frosty, for the jumping — and later I would join her to get the obstinate, brush-shy Bridgit, groomed. The boys never helped in any way, they were too busy snoozing. Saturday mornings were set aside for their late slumbers.

All the tack had been cleaned the night before. Diane and Shirley would usually help — Friday evenings my kitchen would be a hive of industry. My two ironing-boards were used to set the saddles over, and numerous bowls of water would stand on the twin draining boards or on a conveniently-placed chair. Bars of saddle soap, sponges and polishing rags, Brasso! Silvo! and brushes littered the floor. Everywhere you looked there was some kind of cleaning gear. Even the kitchen table would be covered with bridles in pieces, and stacked stirrups soaking, and leather cheek-straps and girths hanging over the backs of chairs.

All the while the coffee pot for most of the evening, gurgled and plopped on the stove, refreshing the busy bees who scrubbed and polished the evening away.

After they'd gone and I'd cleaned up the mess I wondered if it was all worth while. But when I saw the girls riding the lap of honour with their rosettes proudly displayed, somehow the hard work took a back seat and I was filled with a sense of pride. The horses did splendidly, and with the help of the girls they came home with many trophies, they never came back empty handed.

A good deal of the credit mind you, went to Irene, as over the stables by dawn's early light the horse's glorification would begin.

There would be manes to be brushed, plaited and tied. Tails to be pulled, then plaited and bandaged to keep them clean.

Their coats to be washed, brushed legs to be bandaged, feet to be scraped out and hoof oil applied. After all that, they were covered with a horse blanket. This, you hoped, would prevent them from marking their coats, until you could find the time to get yourself ready.

For the Gymkhana events, a tweed hacking jacket, hard hat, long or short boots, jodhpurs, white shirt and black tie, were the usual attire, but for showing and dressage, that was another code of dress.

The jacket then, would have to be of fine cloth, either in black, green, or navy blue, the hard hat to be of the same colour as the jacket. Beige or white jodhpurs tucked into long riding boots for adults, and short leather jodhpur boots for children.

A white shirt, black tie and yellow riding gloves completed the ensemble. For show-jumping the rider carried a whip, and for the showing class, a riding crop or special show-stick would be carried.

Now that you've got yourself and your horse presentable, unless you're hacking to a show — the next thing to do is to get your mount into the horse box. Sometimes, it wasn't that easy ... You can always get an awkward one — usually if you're pressed for time, or you are not too sure of the show's exact location.

Then loading-up-time, would sound something like this ...

"Hold her head still! Get beside her! Don't let her back up! Hold her steady! That's right. Go around to the other side. Take the rope with you!"

There followed a typical yelling match from Bertie, to anyone that was brave enough, or close enough — and who didn't mind being squashed, or trodden on by a hefty-plonked-down hoof on their foot.

All knowledge of that kind of conversation I acquired second-hand.

I, always kept well out of the way on those occasions.

However, once at the show-grounds I would make my way towards the gymkhana ring, where I took great delight in watching the young riders manoeuvre their ponies in all kinds of games.

Such as the sack race; and Gretna Green ... Where a lone rider would gallop to a certain point up-field, pick up a passenger to sit up behind them, then gallop off post haste back to the starting point. I think the ponies enjoyed this as much as the children.

Of all the events I thought the musical sacks were the most fun.

Sometimes, I would participate in the senior's class, much to the amusement of my family and friends.

For this event, competitors had to ride around in a large circle where a number of sacks were placed on the ground inside the ring, one sack to each competitor — less one.

The music that blared forth for the event was relayed from a very weird contraption, it consisted of a microphone attached to an antiquated year of the ark gramophone, and when the music stopped, the idea was that the rider should leap down from the saddle and plonk themselves on the nearest sack.

That's how it was supposed to be done, but in my case, before I could alight from my lofty position, Bridgit, would stop, pick up the sack in her teeth, then cran her neck around so I could grab it from her jaws without moving from the saddle.

A neat trick if we could have pulled it off — but there were too many spectators, and to the delight of the onlookers, if Bridgit failed to gain a sack, she still wanted to stay in the ring, and it was the devil's own job to get her out.

I can't ever recall winning a prize in that event, but it was fun anyway, and it always caused a laugh.

All the show grounds had a refreshment tent of sorts, where one could buy sandwiches, chips, soft drinks, coffee, tea and so on. I usually found myself heading for that place of nourishment before too long, and because there was no one kind enough to mind Bridgit, she tagged along too.

This was courting disaster, because, while I was occupied choosing and paying for my fare, Madam would seize the opportunity to snatch anything she fancied within reach, demolishing the items and the paper bags they were in.

There was never a dull moment spent in her company. We shared lollipops, ice-cream, apples and candy. All I had to say was ' "Do you want some Bridgee." She would stamp her front hoof three times, her ears would shoot forward, and around would come her big, shaggy head, and with her mouth opened wide, down would go the tid-bit and almost my fingers too.

She was a kind and gentle soul once bridled, but on the hunting field, that was another story ...

After a few years of hacking, for that's all she would do, no way could she be persuaded to try her prowess at show-jumping, and so after a lengthy discussion with our local blacksmith, who was the proud possessor of a seventeen-hand thoroughbred stallion — we decided to try our luck by putting the mare in foal.

With the help of the stallion, of course.

So, the next time the mare came into season off she went to the blacksmith's stables, to meet, and we hoped, to mate with Mr. Kelly's illustrious stallion.

She was there a month or so, which cost us a pretty penny for her board and lodgings. A mating fee would be paid later.

That was only if there was a result from that union.

The agreement was — No foal! No fee! Leaving you to try again if and when, she was more compatible. Or, you could save yourself the effort and money by forgetting the whole affair and buy yourself another horse.

I well remember the afternoon that we took Bridgit to the stallion.

It was so wet and cold that we didn't bother to hang around too long, just long enough to take a peep at the handsome bridegroom-to-be. A fine looking stallion of seventeen-hands, with a coat of light grey, a proud head, long neck and back and strong hindquarters.

"He's a lovely fellah!" said Mr. Kelly.

"He should sire a good foal, I hope you get a colt!"

"I hope so to," said Bertie, I could almost see the pound-note signs shining in Berti's eyes, as he was probably calculating how much money he could make if he raised a stallion to sire.

So off we went home, with Bert feeling very pleased with himself.

We were told later, that Bridgit had been a very willing partner in the mating, so I don't know why the blacksmith kept her there so long, but as Bertie put it.

"She had better be in foal, I'm not a millionaire! I can't afford to pay that again."

"It's no good carrying on at me if she isn't," I said, "you should have a private word in the stallion's ear, by the size of our family, perhaps you could have given him some advice."

My spouse ignored the last remarks.

The next time our jovial-Irish blacksmith came over to shoe Bridgit, Frosty and Speedy, I said to him.

"Would you like to come over to the house for a spot of lunch when we've finished?" (I was the one who had to hold the horses).

"Sure, M'dear," he said. "I'd love to, just as soon as I've finished shoeing 'My Big, Irish Gal'." This was his pet name for Bridgit. Then he said, as he gave me a knowing wink.

"You know I 'allus like a drink before tackling the little fellah!"

I knew what he meant, the little drink he referred to, was a wee drop of whisky.

I always thought he deserved it .... because the little fellah he spoke of, was sometimes called by much harsher names, such as. "Little Bugger! Little Beast! and Holy Terror! — Poor Speedy — he hated to be shod, in fact, he hated everything that was done to him.

At shoeing-time he would struggle, squirm and kick, and even try to bite. He would fall to the ground, almost pulling Mr. Kelly down on top of him, and sometimes Mr. Kelly would have to put a twitch on Speedy's nose.

This would make Speedy's eyes roll up in terror, then Mr. Kelly would shout at him. "Holy Mary! Mother of God! I'll wring your blasted neck in a minute."

So you see, that's why I never begrudged Mr. Kelly a drop of the best, in fact, after those ordeals I felt like joining him myself. So I thought, just for this once, I would give him lunch, just as an added bonus. And to tell you the truth I wanted a word in his ear about Bridgit's state of health — foal wise.

Around noon, the blacksmith and I went over to the house for our lunch. I gave him his wee dram and set his meal before him, made a pot of tea, and sat down to eat and talk with him.

He sat thoughtfully munching on his sandwich, then he turned to me and said.

"Now Missus! About Bridgit, have you noticed any change in her yet?"

"No," I said. "Should I have done, she doesn't seem to be getting any bigger! But with Bridgit, it's hard to tell, she's a big girl anyway!''

"Well, if I were you, Missus, I'd get a sample of her urine, and get off to the vet's with it, he'll soon tell 'ya if she's in foal or not. I should do it as soon as you can, then, if she's not, we'll just have to try again.''

"I guess you're right," I said.

I was dying to ask him how to go about getting the urine specimen, but somehow I felt too embarrassed to ask.

I thought to myself, I'll ask Irene, as soon as she gets home. She would be sure to come up with a good solution, so when she came home from work that evening I told her all that the blacksmith had said.

"Wait until Saturday morning," she said. "When I don't have to go to work — we'll try then.''

By Friday evening she came up with a brilliant idea, and early Saturday morning we were over the stables before feeding time.

Irene gave the mare a full bucket of water to drink, we waited patiently until she drank the bucket dry.

Then Irene produced a large clean empty milk bottle from a brown paper bag, and from a pile of straw she pulled out a long, thin strand. Bridgit, looked on with interest ...

"What on earth are you going to do with that piece of straw?" I asked her. "Wait and see," she replied, "Just go and get me another clean bucket.''

I came back with the bucket from Frosty's stable.

"Is this okay?" I said. "Yep!" she replied, "but you'll have to rinse it out first.''

I did as I was bidden, then went back to watch as Irene took her stance by the side of Bridgit's back legs.

"Now you," she said turning to me — "Crouch down and hold this bucket, and be ready to shove it under her rear end when she goes, and for goodness sake don't drop it when she fills it, otherwise, we'll be here all day.''

"I still don't see what the straw's for?" I asked her, as I noticed that she was now leaning forward with the piece of straw clutched tightly in her hand.

"Wait and see," was all she said.

We did wait, and for some considerable time until my arm ached from holding that bucket in such a precarious position.

"She's not going to pass anything," I grumbled. "And I'm not going to stay in this position much longer. What are we going to do?''

"Shush! Be patient," Irene said, "You'll scare the mare. What do you think I've got this straw for?''

"I give up," I said. "What have you got it for?''

"Just you watch," she said. "And have the bucket ready.''

Then to my utter amazement, Irene proceeded to tickle the mare with the straw, right under her lower regions.

"Oh my God!" I said. "Watch out, she'll kick your head in.''

But, surprisingly enough — she didn't.

The tickling worked, and with a wary eye on her back legs I stood my ground, as with a mighty splash! Bridgit, passed her urine. Most of it found its way into the bucket, the rest escaped to splash my trousers and my boots ...ETCETERA! ETCETERA!

I couldn't wait to get into a bath. However, we were highly delighted with our success — until we remembered ..... We still had to get it into the bottle — and, take it to the vet's clinic; and because we were too embarassed to get on the bus with it we walked the three miles to the clinic.

We were afraid to drive a car you see, although we felt perfectly safe on horseback.

We finally arrived at the clinic with the specimen intact, we had a few words with the vet and caught the bus back home.

Some time passed before we had the result and when the letter came we were madly impatient to open it.

"Yes! she was with foal and it would be due some time in May.

The vet's bill, Irene paid, without even showing it to her father, for as she said, "What he didn't know, he wouldn't grieve about, and why spoil our pleasure.''

The vet called again on a number of occasions. When Lady cut her leg, when Speedy developed a severe case of colic. Then, he would have a quick look at Bridgit, too.

"She's coming on fine," he would say.

Our vet had the patience of Job, he was so kind and understanding.

He was a short and chubby man with dark brown eyes and short-cropped brown hair and a swarthy skin, he was a jolly person too. Always ready to laugh at a joke, even when he was asked to visit a sick patient in a wet muddy field, even when he had to climb over a five-barred gate, because I had forgotten to bring the key.

Everyone, spoke highly of him, although I often wondered what he thought about me, I must have been a real eye-opener.

I remembered the first time I accompanied him to the fields at Hook End — he was going to give Speedy an injection.

It took me some time to catch the little horror, then I had more trouble trying to get his head collar on.

I apologized to the vet for keeping him waiting, as I pulled and tugged Speedy along to where the vet stood.

"That's perfectly all right," he said. Then he smiled, and that smile turned into hearty laughter.

"What's the joke?" I said.

"I don't like to tell you," he replied. "But no wonder he doesn't want that collar on — you've got it on upside down."

I felt such a fool, I wished the ground would open up and swallow me.

"Never mind," he said. "We all have to learn," and from then on we became friends, and over the years he was always there for us, in all weather's and in times of stress.

No doctor that I ever knew was as quick to attend his patients as that dedicated man. After a while I think he recognized my voice easily, for when I telephoned him he knew straightaway who it was, and when we told him about Bridgit, he said.

"There's no need to worry! She's a strong healthy mare, and there should be no trouble at all. You know," he continued, "May will come around in no time at all."

The great day finally came, and on a Sunday morning early in May, Bridgit presented us with a fine colt foal, but not in the clean warm stable. Oh no!

That mare, chose the muckiest place in the field, behind the stables at the foot of the manure pile, and in the pouring rain.

I'm afraid I was not there to witness it, but an urgent phone call from our friend Arthur, whose garden backed on to the field, told us he had seen it all, while he was picking mushrooms.

Trust my luck! To go through all that anxiety and then miss the most thrilling part.

The call sent Irene, Carl, Tony and Laurence, scuttling over to the stables, with Bertie well to the fore.

They were armed with buckets of hot water, my best clean bath towels, and some hot mash. As soon as they went, I made a frantic telephone call to the vet.

I dialed the number, fidgeting about in nervous agitation while I waited. It seemed like ages before anyone answered, at last I heard a familiar voice.

"Veterinary surgeon here! Mr. Armstrong speaking, what can I do for you?" he asked.

"I've just had a foal," I said.

For a moment the line went silent as I suddenly realized what I had said. Mr. Armstrong I knew had treated a great number of horses over the years, but I don't think he had ever had one telephone him before.

So I wasn't surprised when I detected a slight hint of humour in his voice when he replied.

"Oh! And when was this?" he asked.

"I'm not sure," I said, "I wasn't there at the time, I was in the kitchen cooking breakfast."

"How awkward," he replied.

"All I know is," I continued, "That it was born early this morning behind the manure pile; and my neighbour — actually saw it happen."

"How embarrassing for you," he replied. "I hope you're all right now, anyway, what do you want me to do about it?"

"I'd like you to come over as soon as you can." I said. "Just to be on the safe side."

"Has the afterbirth come away yet?" He said.

"I'm not sure, I never asked," I said nervously.

"Are you sure you're okay?" he asked once again.

"Yep! I'm fine," I told him. I could hear him laughing, then he paused awhile before he went on to say.

"Ah! Ha! By the panic you were in I thought at first it was you that had a baby."

"No thanks," I said. "I've had enough babies, NO, it was Bridgit. Please forgive me for the mix up, I am so excited."

"That's okay," he said. "Now let me see, it's Mrs. Holden isn't it, from Glovers Field?"

"Yes!" I said. "That's right."

"That's fine," he replied. "I'll be over to see the new mother as soon as possible."

I was still laughing when I went over to the stables to see the new arrival for myself. Thank goodness the vet was used to me and that he had a great sense of humour.

The first six months Mare and Foal were in the home fields together, the other horses were moved to the big fields at Hook End behind Blackmore House.

The two of them were inseparable, the spirited foal would caper and cavort in front and behind his dam wherever she went.

She, the proud dam, would toss her head and run along with him, they made a charming picture ...

The foal, whom I named Smoky, had the same markings as the Mare, but there the likeness ended.

For he was tall and rangy and had the makings of a seventeen-hand hunter, just like his sire.

The colour of his short silky-haired coat was a soft grey, akin to smoke. His tail and mane were sparse and as black as jet. His eyes were large and inquiring, soft and deep as liquid pools.

He didn't seem at all scared when I approached him, and when I petted him he made no special effort to move away. In fact, I think he thoroughly enjoyed it.

Irene had an in-hand halter made for him in fine leather, it was adorned with tiny, brass eyelets and studs. When he had it on, he looked real cute. Wearing it with pride, he would stand by the fence with Bridgit, waiting to be admired by the village folk.

He also became a show-piece for the patrons of the Swan Inn.

Bridgit didn't mind people looking — and if she managed to scrounge a tid-bit from the audience, so much the better, but God help anyone who tried to invade her privacy by trying to climb the fence — that was another matter.

No tid-bit was worth her foal being harmed, she must have thought, as she headed him off to the other end of the field.

When the six months were up, it was time for the mare and foal to be separated. Smoky to stay in the home field until he was gelded, and his dam to go back to the big fields to join Cobber, Speedy and Frosty.

Lady Jane came back, to keep the little foal company.

There, she was affectionately known as Aunt Jane, as she was forever fussing over the young foal.

Smoky was upset at losing his dam and for the first few days he went off his food, but by the end of that month, he was to be seen tucking-in greedily away, with his head deep down in his food bin, and life went on as usual in that horsey world of ours.

# Chapter Nine

# RIDER IN FLIGHT

Now at this stage of my life, nineteen-seventy-one, we were the proud owners of, Lady Jane Grey, Speedy, Frosty and Bridgit, and of course the little foal, Smoky; and during those past few years the family, had also increased.

Irene, was still single and living at home, as were sons Anthony, Laurence, Geoffrey and Ray, although Anthony and his girlfriend Patricia, were thinking of tying the matrimonial knot in the fall of nineteen-seventy-two.

Carl had been married for five years to Mary a local girl, and they had two children. Tracy, my first grandchild, born in nineteen-sixty-seven, and her brother Gary, born two years after, and it was at this time that I suddenly began to feel very tired, old age creeping on, or was it something to do with being a grandmother. Whatever it was I felt it was time I had a rest.

Now every housewife deserves a break at sometime or other, and this housewife was certainly due for one. Who could deny me, twenty-eight years of wedded bliss, nose constantly to the grindstone, and without a holiday for years.

I mentioned this sorry state of affairs when I next saw my friend Rose, she was a world-wide traveller.

"Why don't you go over to Canada to see Bert's family for a holiday," she said.

"I'm sure they would love to see you, and I know where you can get a reduced-rate flight."

"Go on, Rose," I said. "It sounds interesting."

"Well," she said, "You have to join the Canadian-Overseas-Club first, I joined last year just before I went to see my sister."

"Are you sure I can join?" I said. "Sure," she said.

"Anyone with relatives over there can and as your husband's an ex-Canadian Serviceman, all the better."

"I had a smashing time over there, I'm sure you'll love it." "I'll show you my photos next time I come over." "Okay," I said. "That's fine."

Then I listened with renewed interest as she described the many places she had visited and the wondrous sights she had seen.

"It all sounds fine Rose." I said. "But I don't think Bert will take kindly to the idea of me being away from home for four weeks on my own, you know we both can't go, he can't leave his business all that time."

I couldn't see him lashing out the air fare for two tickets anyway, as much as he would have liked to have gone to visit his family.

"Anyway, I'll ask him," I said. "He can only say no."

Then I thought about the family and I wondered who I could persuade to do the chores, so later that evening, after I'd served Bertie with his favourite meal, I approached the subject of the long-distance holiday. He sat thoughtfully sipping his tea, I sat waiting for the answer and I nearly fell off the chair when he said.

"I don't see why not if the fare's reasonable, it's time you had a break anyway." Then he said. "As Rose put the idea into your head, she..... can help out."

The cooking and the cleaning would pose no problems for Rose, for she was an excellent housewife, but when I stopped to think of some of the other chores she would be expected to do I shuddered, and it was then that I realized that she had no experience at all with horse-flesh of any kind..... ALIVE OR DEAD... and when I mentioned her kind offer to help in the home, the boys said. "No thanks Mum, we'll do those jobs, ourselves." Heaven forbid, whatever made me think they could, but my heart was now so set on this never-to-be-forgotten solo adventure, that I took their word for it.

"You had better find out all about it... soon.. Mum," they said. "Before we change our minds."

So the very next morning when all the family had vacated the house, and the four-legged creatures had been fed, I sat down to write a letter to the Canadian Overseas Club, and had the nerve to enquire for the particulars of their reduced-rate trip. I asked for the times and the place of departure, and any other general information I thought I might need. Then I sat back in a chair with a nice cup of tea to fantasize on the wonderful things that I might be doing in a few months time.

Like lazing around in the sun, with no stables to clean, no horses to muck-out and feed, no shirts to iron, (I usually ironed sixty of them each week).

Mind you, I'd never flown before..... at least not in a jetliner. I'd often flown through the air from off a horse's back.

I finished my tea, came out of my daydreaming, to reality.

What was I going to wear? I could hardly go in riding gear, and my wardrobe was sadly lacking in clothes suitable for a fancy holiday, most of my time was spent in riding breeches and boots, and I didn't think the flight attendants would take too kindly to a passenger that wore spurs.

Was all this wishful thinking?

However a few weeks later I did receive a letter from the club, with an application form to join, and to my surprise there was also an application form and all the information for the Canadian Holiday.

The letter made my day and when I showed it to the family they immediately set to work to make their plans.

Did I detect an urgency in their generous offer to help me refurbish my wardrobe and help with my expenses? If I did, I never said a word. I just wondered what they were planning to get up to. Although maybe I did say. "Thanks very much. It will all help."

I sent the money off for the ticket and the subscription for the club as soon as I could, just in case one of the boys changed his mind and found a better use for it.

The rest of the cash I spent on a new outfit. A yellow wool dress and coat, some shoes and a large suitcase, and a few lengths of dress material from the market.

All you could hear in the house for the next few weeks, was the WHIRR! WHIRR! BUZZ! BUZZ! of the sewing machine as I churned out homemade fashions in which to bedeck myself for the forthcoming trip.

The flight ticket and all the other info arrived in good time, but my suitcase had been packed ages before, in case I forgot something .... that's the sort of person I am, always ready miles before time, and as my husband used to say as I always set the breakfast table before retiring.

"Why don't we eat breakfast now?" I would quickly answer back, "I know of someone not sitting too far away from me, that would," Looking in his direction.

The day before I was due to cross the ocean to a distant shore, Irene, bought me a new saddle for Frosty, I wanted to try it out straightaway.

"Nothing doing," she said.

"If you come a cropper and fall off, Dad will kill me."

Now as it happened Anthony and Patricia were going to a show in London that evening, so they offered to drive me to London and to see me safely settled in a hotel for the night.

One preferably near Gatwick Airport.

We found such a hotel, small but clean, and the Italian couple the proprietors were kind and very helpful, they took the trouble to prepare a delicious meal for me but I never ate a thing, and I never slept a wink either. I stood by the open window for most of the night gazing out at the starlit skies, thinking.......

I suppose the family had thought that my being next to the airport would stop me worrying about missing my flight.

There was no need, I was there in plenty of time, and it's a small wonder I never parked myself beside the runway in the middle of the night.

I had already phoned the organizer several times in the past week, asking what he probably considered, stupid questions. When I met that patient and long-suffering man at the airport, after I had introduced myself, he remarked ....

"I am pleased to meet you, but you have surprised me, by our telephone conversations I had imagined you to be a much older woman." "Ah! Hem! Well........"

He hesitated finding it hard to put into words no doubt exactly what else he wanted to say to me.

Perhaps he had expected someone more feeble and frail of body, and I'd surprised him, by looking so healthy, so maybe he thought I was a little feeble on top especially after all those questions I had previously asked him over the telephone.

So without further ado he just gave me a cheeky grin and with a slight chuckle in his voice he said....

"The rest of our group are over there, please... keep close to them and I'll get back to you before takeoff."

"Don't get lost," he said, as he dashed away presumably to look for any further strays, possibly praying, that there would be no more like me.

We boarded the aircraft in due course, we were greeted by some of the members of the crew all looking as neat as a new pin in their smart uniforms, they helped us find our seats and safely stowed our suitcases and duty-free goods in the luggage racks above. I had a seat next to the window and a couple I had become friendly with sat in the two seats behind me.

They had flown before so I was glad, I thought if I got scared at least I would have a friendly face to turn to.

When we were all seated and made comfortable with air-pillows and so forth, we were told to adjust our seatbelts, put out any cigarettes and sit comfortably. Then a voice from a hidden speaker announced that we would soon be ready for takeoff.

The roar of the engines and the swift forward surge as we took off scared me half to death, but, being a curious person by nature and wanting to see what the world looked like from way on high I had opted for a window seat when booking, solely for that reason. It was a mistake in more ways than one.

For as the vast vehicle rose steeply up into the brilliant sunshine I caught my first glimpse of the fast disappearing earth below and it made me feel quite sick.

The effect wore off eventually as the novelty of being one of the Jet-Set took over.

We hadn't been airborne very long before the chief air-stewardess and her assistant came to our cabin and stood in the centre isle.

"This," said the gentleman in the seat beside me, "Is time for the safety drill routine."

"Gosh," I said to him, "I hadn't thought of any danger."

In fact I had been so busy for the last ten minutes prying into the pocket-container fixed to the back of the seat in front of me, that other thoughts had gone flying out of the window. The flying package was so interesting.

There was a glossy magazine full of pictures depicting fashionable models in fine array, a whole page and a half devoted to duty-free goods which could be obtained on board. A book containing a map indicating the flight's route across the Atlantic, and two coloured picture-postcards of the aircraft itself. A Freddie Laker Special, a Boeing 707. There was also a large paper bag, I thought it was for the rubbish, evidently it was not.... but for fliers who couldn't keep their goodies down. All explained in the pamphlet.

There was also another pamphlet full of pictures and instructions, as to where the nearest escape outlets were, and the quickest way to leave the aircraft should the engines fail or the wings drop off. I was busily engaged in studying this and contemplating on what I would do if ever the situation presented itself, when the voice of the stewardess claimed my attention.

"Listen very carefully," she said. "And watch closely."

"This is your life jacket, and your life may depend on it."

"It is for your safety."

This all looked rather intriguing, and when she mentioned the word, Safety.... I thought I had better sit up and take notice.

She held the article up for all to see, then she said.

"You fix it onto your back and tie the tapes so, once it's in place it is then ready to inflate, and you blow into the mouthpiece.... so"

Good thing she didn't have to blow for as her mouth went over the tube piece, I began to laugh.

"Its not funny," she said lifting her head and looking straight across at me.

"No it isn't," I said.

"Sorry, it's just my thoughts."

But I wasn't going to repeat them to her, not in front of all those people. I was just thinking to myself, I might be able to tie the thing on but would I have enough puff left to blow it up especially after eating, the peanuts, the snacks, the lunch and the tea, not to mention the complimentary drinks that were promised us in the brochure.

I dreaded to think what chance I would have of surviving should I have to bail-out as I had enough trouble trying to blow up a balloon. So I controlled my mirth when the stewardess demonstrated how to use the oxygen mask.

Later I tried to snatch forty winks, no chance. As all kinds of uniformed girls and guys hovered over and about us.

"Would you care for a drink?" was the first inquiry.

"Yes! that would be very nice... thank you," I said. Then I thought, suppose I arrive at my destination TIPSY!? Whatever would my Mother-in-law think of me? My usual excuse for a drink was nervous disorder, well! there was never a more nervous person than me on the plane that day.

The food never stopped coming, it was either; tea, coffee, peanuts or pop then a full lunch of steaks, fries, jello and ice cream...... I had tried to keep slim for my visit and this abundance of food wasn't going to help any.

There were other exciting things that happened on that trip between drinking and eating. There was the man that insisted on singing the National Anthem after his fill-up on the free drinks, a small boy who spilled his pop into the radio panel, and the old gentleman behind me who insisted the steward get his baggage down almost every half hour, because he thought he'd forgotten his passport. Not to mention a few wild kids that ran up and down the aisles or spent a considerable time monopolizing the toilets. There were also forms to fill in for duty-free goods and landing forms to fill out and, once everyone had found their air-legs so to speak, they walked up and down the aisles chattering to their fellow passengers.

It was all very splendid and everything went fine, the time went so fast and it surprised me when I heard the pilot's voice come over the intercom when he said....

"Ladies and Gentlemen, we are now flying over Montreal and we will be landing in Toronto very soon, let me take this opportunity to welcome you to Canada."

"I hope you all had a very pleasant trip."

He then gave out the altitude and the weather report for Toronto. Then, as an afterthought, he added.

"Did you all remember to alter your watches?"

Everyone laughed. Four hours later when the time-change took effect they would all very likely be yawning, not laughing. I know I was.

It was a beautiful sunny afternoon when we touched-down at the Lester Pearson Airport and as we taxied into the terminal I could see aircraft displaying the flags of many nations, also the planes of Canadian air companies with their Maple Leaf emblems. Some were preparing for takeoff, others, like ours, were in the process of unloading, the whole place was a hive of industry.

I was so engrossed watching the comings and goings that I had failed to notice what the other passengers were doing.

When suddenly a hand tapped me on the shoulder and a voice from behind said......

"It's okay now, you can unfasten your seat belt, we have landed."

"Yes! I gathered that," I said.

Then I was asked if I needed any help to get my hand-luggage down.

"No! that's fine," I said, "I think I can manage."

My two new friends of the trip who were bound for Vancouver said.

"We'll have to say goodbye to you now as we have to hurry to catch the connecting flight, hope you have a good holiday and we'll see you here in four weeks time."

"Yep! sure," I said, as I turned to reach up for the couple of tote bags stashed away in the luggage rack.

Clutching the bags tightly I joined in with the rest of the passengers who were pushing and shoving each other in their efforts to be the first to embark.

I wondered what all the rush was about, I soon found out when I found myself at the end of the line at the customs barrier.

*Phil on Jumping Jody in Canada*

This was going to take quite a time I thought, as I had heard about custom official's questions from Rose, but I wasn't prepared for the length of the line-up waiting to pass through, or for some of the, what I thought of as stupid questions they asked me...... Like......

"How long are you staying?"

Boy! and I had only just arrived, there's a welcome. "Have you any plants, fresh meat or sausages?"

Cricky! I'd had enough trouble lugging around a suitcase and my bottle of Duty-free Whisky, then I thought, surely it's not the custom in Canada to take your own food and I didn't think Canada had any rationing problems.

I told the customs guy..... "No!"

But I couldn't resist when he asked me the next question.

"Have you any steak?"

"No!" I said, "It's too expensive in England, so I put a few pounds of HORSE-FLESH... in my suitcase instead."

He never even smiled. Perhaps he believed me.

He let me go through anyway and with an unexpected parting shot he said.

"Have a good day."

"Thanks," I said "I will, that's if I ever get out of the airport."

After the customs inquisition it was time to collect my luggage.

It was only one suitcase... more like a trunk...

However I almost had a fight on my hands when trying to gain lawful possession of it from the carousel. What a performance that was.

I am used to it all now, but little did I know then that I would be making this selfsame journey the very next year and ten times more until I finally settled in the land that I was about to tread for the very first time.

However the next thing I had to find was a trolley to hump my possessions on, then find how to get out of the place, and to find someone willing to claim me.......

The exit doors loomed ahead, but where were the handles?, not on the sides of the doors, that was for sure.

I looked around for some fellow traveller to instruct me, or do the "Open Sesame" routine, I glanced upwards, as if expecting help from that direction, no luck, but there on the other side of the glass partition was a very tall young man, he was nodding his head and waving his arms around like he was trying to convey something to me. Then, he started to jump sideways pointing his fingers towards the floor, he then commenced to do an imitation of the breast-stroke like a swimmer. I looked at him in disbelief... SWIM for it, no he can't mean that, anyway I can't swim.

While I was trying to figure out his meaningful signs, a kind soul spotting my predicament stepped in to save me as he whispered in my ear.....

"If you stand in the centre of the rubber mat, just here," he indicated. "The doors will open automatically, see."

The clever man stood on the mat and abracadabra the doors slid back noiselessly, providing me with an escape route to my worried-looking foreign relative.

I had wanted so much to make a good first impression, but once again had been the joker.... as always.

There were smiles, hugs, and kisses all round, from my brother-in-law and a family friend whom I had met before.

I was relieved of my heavy suitcase and asked to accompany him to the terminal's car park.

"The car's upstairs," he said.

"It's on the top floor, I hope you're not afraid of heights?"

"Only of tall horses," I said. But I don't think he heard me. As we reached the lift to ascend to the top floor my brother-in-law informed me (with much pride in his voice) that he had just bought himself a new car, "I do hope you'll like it," he said.

We stepped out of the lift and made our way over to the treasured vehicle, he stowed the luggage away in the trunk and I waltzed around to the other side to get in.

"Sorry," he said. "but I can't let you drive her yet, round to the other side you go."

"Oh yes, silly me," I said. "You drive on the wrong side over here, don't you?"

"Anyway, your car's quite safe with me, I don't drive." I dashed around to the other side of his brand-spanking-new car, grabbed the handle, gently mind you, then, Horror upon Horror, the dratted thing came off in my hand.

I gazed at him in disbelief, I didn't know whether to laugh or cry as I stared up into his chalk-white face.

Now whether he thought he was going to be entertaining the bride of Frankenstein I had no idea, but judging by the look on his face and the lack of any sound issuing forth from his lips, I suspected he was in some kind of shock.

However, seeing that I was rather upset he tried to put a bold front on the incident and tried to make a joke of the whole situation, just to put me at ease.

Finding some string in the trunk of the car he proceeded to tie the door of the car up.... very tightly, probably to ensure that I didn't escape...to do any more damage.

I have since, often wondered what he said to his wife about our first encounter.

Lawrence was a friendly chap who hailed from Manitoba, he was generous and kind, and he was good enough to escort me in his handle-repaired car to many places of interest, including the "Western Fair" in London, Ontario. There, I was in my element, especially when they had a chuck-wagon race, I cheered the horses until I was hoarse. During the whole of my stay in Canada the family treated me like royalty and Bertie's uncle took me to Niagara Falls, where we spent a most enjoyable weekend.

After a week of seeing the sights, I was asked if I would like to visit Lawrence's sister.

She keeps horses you know," he said.

"Would you like to go and see her?"

I needed no second invitation.

"When!" I said.... "When!"

"I'll phone her as soon as she gets home from work," he said.

He did.... and I was asked to stay with her for the following weekend. So the next Saturday morning I packed my riding boots and the rest of the gear, which I had conveniently bought with me, just in case, and we set off.

I just couldn't miss this golden opportunity that had presented itself to me. So the second weekend of my stay in Canada found me all dressed up in my English riding ensemble, ready to do battle with any horse that was made available to me.

I hoped I wouldn't let the side down..... What!.

His sister's place was way out of town in a small village called Browns Corner, in Perth County.

We drove in silence for awhile, I admiring the scenery. Then Lawrence said.

"There's the house at the top of that hill."

He turned the car into a wide-upsweeping laneway, more of a track really. Its surface was of hard-packed earth, dry and very dusty, clouds of thick dust swirled up and around the car forcing Lawrence to close the windows.

Through the dust I could just make out the fields that bordered the track, and a row of white-painted wagon wheels that stood like sentinels on each side.

About halfway up the quarter-of-a-mile track stood a large log cabin and as we drove slowly past it Lawrence explained...

"Isn't that just dandy?, it belongs to my niece, her friend built it — and," he drawled "It's all done out in Western Style. Her friend is a Texan. You'll be able to see it all for yourself tomorrow, you're invited there for chuck."

"That's nice," I said. "I'll look forward to that."

We continued on until we reached the top of the hill where he stopped the car by the side of a large barn.

"Now, before we go into the house to meet the folks," he said. "There's some fine looking fellahs I'd like you to meet."

This could be fun I thought. He took my arm and steered me over towards the barn, and there, just behind it was a large corral where three handsome horses in full Western Tack stood quietly waiting. The rangy sorrel I was told was a quarter-horse and his name was "Hank".

"A Quarter-horse — whatever's that," I asked as I gave it a perplexed stare.

A tall guy came out from the barn and sauntered over.

"Hi," he said. "I guess you're the gal from England. I guess you don't have quarter-horses there?"

"Well, if they do — I've never heard of them," I replied.

He laughed ........

"What about this little bay gelding here?" I asked.

"Oh he belongs to Debbie — a friend."

So this was the Texan I thought, the accent was unmistakable.

"This h'a fellah's just stabled here, but I guess you have the owner's permission to ride him — that's why he's tacked up and ready to roll. In fact, you can ride either of them, they're all safe for a novice to ride."

He turned to re-enter the barn and as a parting shot, he said.

"I'll see you later, when I've finished m'a chores."

I pondered on what he'd said about a novice, the nerve of the guy, novice indeed! I'd show him.

I turned my attention back to the horses again to study their tack.

The western bridles — had bits such as I had never seen before. They were called, so I was informed, a mechanical-hackamore, they had no contact with the horse's mouth but rested under their chin like an up-turned stirrup and just covered one ear. The saddles looked hard and uncomfortable, and the stirrups were away down too low, and the stirrup irons which were made of wood were encased in hand-tooled leather, and the cinch was tied with the ends tucked in, nothing like an English girth, a broad leather band buckled with a three-way prong on either side of the saddle covered by a small protection flap of leather. All this I noticed with mounting trepidation before I was called into the house to meet the folks.

After the introductions and friendly handshakes all round, I was asked if I would like to change into my riding clothes and join Jim, Paula's friend, at the corral. I changed in double-quick time and ran as fast as I could to where the Texan waited.

"Which horse would you like to ride?" I was asked by my host Harry, Lawrence's brother-in-law, a tall bespectacled man in his prime years.

"I don't mind," I said.

Did he detect a slight tremor in my voice when I answered him?

I wonder if he saw my knees shaking as I stood there trying to imagine how I was going to get up that far to the saddle by way of those very long stirrups. Why had no one mentioned that I was expected to ride Western?

By that time other spectators had gathered at the corral, some had the foresight to bring their cameras. It seemed that my antics on these animals were to be recaptured for posterity, or, to be saved for a laugh on wet boring evenings.

The motley crowd had already taken up their positions for the viewing of my prowess as a rider, or, my downfall if disaster overtook me. It didn't deter me in any way, as with a defiant shrug of the shoulders I walked boldy over to pat the roan "Jumping Jody".

"I'll try this lad," I said, encouraged by his quiet stance, he was smaller than the Sorrel, so I thought he might be easier to manage, and not such a great height to fall from.

I was to be accompanied by my host's daughter who was mounted on Hank, and Debbie who sat astride her own horse Shawn, and, as I mounted Jumping Jody, Paula looked across at me and assured me all would be fine. And so it proved to be ....

After the photographic session the three of us set off on our trusty steeds for an enjoyable hack through the surrounding countryside. There was no bother, I never stumbled down a gopher-hole, or came down hard on the horn of the saddle, and I even managed to post, lope and gallop, I was so pleased and when the girls suggested that we do another tour the following day I was happy to comply.

I could go into more details pertaining to my visit, hour by hour, day by day, but the riding that weekend stayed in my mind forever to be told over and over again. I enjoyed it more than any other adventure on that momentous trip.

Sunday, was a beautiful day, not a cloud in the sky, the perfect day for riding. The girls chuckled as they fitted me out in Western garb. From her mother, Paula borrowed a bright-mauve silk shirt, matching pants and a large cowboy hat. The pointed cowboy boots were too narrow for my wide, outsized feet, so I had to make do with my own black riding boots.

They didn't show, because the trousers were too long as the girls mother to whom the outfit belonged was extraordinarily tall, so a few swift alterations had to be made, or I would have stood on the trouser-legs — not the easiest way to mount a horse — with so much dangling.

Pride and sheer perseverance must have glued me to that saddle, I retained my dignity, in walk, lope and gallop.

The girls were so pleased that I had taken to Western riding so well, that for the next few weeks I had the pleasure of going to and taking part in various riding events.

Showing, Pleasure Riding and Barrel racing, and a few rides out with the master of the stables.

So all was forgiven, whatever I did silly on Terra-firma I certainly made up for it when out riding, so my self esteem was restored. And, as if to make me feel even happier I received a letter from Bertie, to say that our dear Frosty had challenged and beaten all comers in the show-jumping ring, and winning the Southend Challenge Cup, clearing a five-feet-three inches jump, no mean feat for a fourteen-hand pony.

So after a month of wonderful times and fond memories, I left those far off shores to be welcomed back home by friends and family and my dear old stable mates.

# Chapter Ten

# TO MATE A NANNY GOAT

At this point in time I would like you to visualize this picture of Essex. A County steeped in history, with many fine old churches, such as St. Thomas the Apostle in Navestock, where my eldest son was married.

This beautiful church was built in the twelfth century, its timbered belfry and west tower were the pride of the surrounding countryside, as was the country seat of the Lord of The Manor at Brizes Park.

Picture in spring the fields upturned by the ploughman, a cloud of seagulls following in his wake, birds building their nests in tangled hawthorn hedgerows. The long, narrow-winding lanes, beset on both sides by tall stately Oak, Ash and Sycamore, so still and silent, their branches entwined to form a green leafy canopy.

Summer rains and heat hazes; tall poppies blooming, and the glimpse of apples and cherries in the orchards.

Imagine the scene at harvest time, the fields resplendent in oats, wheat, corn and barley; and wild juicy blackberries, nestling between high hedges. Tall haystacks stand golden as the thatched roofs on cottages.

In winter the hedgerows, white from the early morning frost, made colourful by the holly berries and the boughs of mistletoe.

And on the outskirts of Ongar were green acres of prime forest land. And therein was Epping, a fine Market Town.

The town of Epping is one of the most interesting in Southern England... The narrow, cobblestoned streets, walkways, houses, shops and picturesque gardens in the market square go back to medieval times. Several of the Inns date back to the Tudor period, and some of the older inhabitants seemed to be dressed in the fashion of the days of yore too.

On Thursdays and Saturdays merchants were to be found displaying their miscellaneous wares on stalls set up in the market place.

Books, china, glasswear and underwear, dishes, pots and pans, fresh fruit, fish and eggs. The vendors cries were a cross between a plead and a whine, and there was so much shouting as they spouted forth their wares. The square was always crowded with country folk, all intent on finding a bargain. Offsprings clung to their mother's skirts, and babies cried as they tried to escape from their buggies, while their mothers conversed with old friends from the neighbouring farms. My own interest was not entirely in the market and its wares, but rather in the tack shop. I loved the smell from the leather saddles, and it was sheer ecstasy for me to stand and gaze at the many colourful nylon head-collars that hung in bunches suspended from a hook in the ceiling, and just inside the door to tempt the parents of pony-mad children, there stood in the most prominent position of the shop, a rather well-groomed stuffed pony, decked out in the most expensive saddlery.

It looked so lifelike that I was sure some of the children thought it was real.

Now at this stage of our show-jumping era I had very little knowledge of the correct terminology that was used for the special show-jumping equipment, but we all have to learn at sometime, so bearing this in mind I was quite surprised one morning when Irene said to me.

"Mum, do you think you could find the time to go into Epping for me today?" "What for?" I asked.

"Well, I want some brushing boots for Lady, from the tack shop," she said. But before I could answer her the two younger boys had started an argument as to who had whose football socks, I had to stop the argument quickly or they would both have been late for the school bus, so somehow or other I must have misunderstood what Irene had said. But as she said later, she distinctly remembered asking me to get "BRUSHING BOOTS"; but my mind being somewhat distracted by the lads shouting at one another, I thought she said "'RUSSIAN BOOTS".

It never entered my head to ask her what they were for and why they were so called. Russian boots to me were a long rubber boot worn in the rainy season, usually called Wellingtons, so named after the old Duke of Wellington who wore something similar when he rode into battle.

However, I did manage to get some of the conversation correct, especially the part about Epping and the tack shop, and as I told Irene, I would certainly find the time to go there. So, once the boys had gone to school and everything was quiet I hurried with my chores, got myself ready and headed for the Ongar Road bus stop.

I was no stranger to the store as I had been there many times before, once when they made me a special saddle for Bridgit, when we bought Frosty's new saddle; and when I took Raymond to be fitted out for his first riding habit.

I can still remember how his face lit up, when he saw that magnificently attired stuffed pony.

So when I entered the shop that day, I was greeted warmly by the staff with nods and smiles; and a cheery ''Good Morning,'' from the manager; who came over to serve me personally.

''What can I do for you this fine morning?'' he said.

''Ah!'' I replied with a smile. ''There's lots of nice things I can see to-day, that I would very much like to have, but actually I came on behalf of my daughter. She is entering one of our mares for the show-jumping events at Harwood and she asked me to get her a pair of ....RUSSIAN BOOTS....''

''Did she by gad'' said the manager, as he whipped out his pocket hand-kerchief to hold over his mouth.

''Have you got a cold?'' I asked him stepping slightly back.

He seemed to take some time before replying, and as he removed his handkerchief I noticed there were tears in his eyes, and when he saw me staring at him he hastily proceeded to wipe them dry.

''Oh!....No!....No! ...No! ...'' He stammered.

''Please pardon my mirth, but what did you ask me for?''

''A Pair of Russian Boots'' .... I said, peering at him perplexed. ''Why! What's wrong? What's so funny?'' I asked.

''Oh my dear'' he said, taking me by the arm and holding on tight, he was bent over double and killing himself with laughter. ''Sorry,'' he said, ''So sorry, will you please wait here while I go and get the boots, then you'll understand why I was laughing.''

He was gone for some considerable time, and when he finally did ap-pear he was carrying a pair of Wellingtons in one hand, and two curiously-looking grey rubber objects in the other, and without a word being spo-ken he calmly walked over to where the stuffed pony stood. I looked on with interest as he knelt down slowly and proceeded to place the Well-ington boots, one by the side of each back hoof, and the grey objects he put on the pony's front hooves and when he had finished this operation he looked up at me and said. ''Which do you prefer ... The BRUSHING OR THE RUSSIAN?''

Well, I had to laugh, even though I felt a right idiot. I was too lost for words to excuse my blunder and I could feel my cheeks getting hotter and hotter wishing whole heartily that the ground would open up and swallow me.

''Why! you're blushing,'' the manager said. ''I am sorry, but I just couldn't resist the temptation to demonstrate.''

"That's okay," I said. "I'll listen more carefully when next I'm asked to get something from here — If there ever is a next time."

"Oh you'll soon learn about these things," he said.

"I'll try to explain what they're for. These rubber so called boots are made to protect the horse's hooves in the ring, it's to stop them striking their front hooves on the rail of the jump."

"Thank you," I said "for explaining, it seems a jolly good idea, I'll take two sets," for, no way was I going back to that store again, well, not until that amusing episode was long forgotten.

I never did tell the boys, I couldn't have stood the ribbing and I never told Irene, not at that time, but I expect she often wondered why I burst into laughter whenever she put them on Lady Jane. After that episode I decided I wouldn't volunteer to go for any more horsey shopping, at least not until I had learned a little more about this Equestrian business. And the only way to do this I thought was to seriously consider joining a riding school.

It was a few weeks after the tack shop fiasco when I was returning from a short hack on a gloriously sunny afternoon, that I happened quite by chance to meet a charming lady who was to join and encourage me in this new venture.

I was riding Frosty that day, and I thought what a good idea it would be if I rode back home by way of Raymond's school, then he could impress his school chums, by riding the pony home.

I reached the school gates, then complying with the headmaster's wishes that all means of transport should keep clear of the main gates, I dismounted, and took my stance at the far corner of the building well out of harm's way, while still retaining a clear view of the pupil's exits and far enough away from any tempting foliage — Frosty, was rather partial to greenery and flowering shrubs and standing in one position for any length of time was not his favorite pastime, unless of course his jaws could be champing on forbidden fruit.

We stood idly in the warm afternoon's sunshine, gazing at nothing in particular when suddenly I was startled by a voice hailing me from a parked car from across the road. I looked over and saw a blonde, middle-aged lady in a small station wagon, she was leaning halfway out of its open window. She waved her hand in greeting as she addressed me in a very pleasing tone.

"Hello there! May I join you?"

And that was how I came to make the acquaintance of Margaret Mells, an inhabitant of the neighbouring village of Blackmore.

We introduced ourselves, and she told me her name, we stood and chatted for awhile, about the weather, the price of food and the school in general, then she asked me who I was waiting for.

"I'm waiting for my son Raymond," I said. "He is in the top class."

"That's funny," she said. "So is my son Andrew. Do you know him?"

"Well not really," I said. My boys have so many friends that I'm afraid half of the time I don't catch their names."

"Oh my son Andrew often talks about your son Raymond," she said "And he mentioned about Ray's pony, he's called Speedy, isn't he?"

"Yes," I said "that's right, we also have Frosty, who you see here, and some other horses too; my daughter and I do most of the riding.

"How lucky you are," she said. "I wish my husband would buy me a horse, and so does my daughter Nessa, she's potty about them. She helps out at the Norton Heath Riding School you know and I often go there to have a few lessons."

"Strange you should say that," I told her. "I was thinking of taking a few lessons there myself, but I don't drive, so it would be rather difficult for me to get there."

"Oh I could come for you and take you over there," she said. "No trouble at all." "Would you really," I said. "That would be most kind. What about a little compromise?" I helpfully suggested, "If you take me to Norton Heath, I'll let you come riding with me sometime, on one of our horses."

I wondered how she would get along with Bridgit.

"Great," she said. "I'll look forward to that, what about us arranging something for next week? And about the lessons, you leave it to me and I'll have a word with Nessa, she'll fix you up with some lessons at the school and as soon as she makes the arrangements I'll phone you, and let you know all the details."

After we had sorted that little plan out, Margaret made a great fuss of Frosty who lapped it all up like a cat with a saucer of cream.

The whistle blew and out of the school the boys came trooping. Ray, was the last one out as usual, with his tie all askew and tucked under one ear, his shoe laces untied, and his socks, one up and one down, a typical boy. He was pleased to see me and his eyes lit up when he saw Frosty, and he needed no second invitation when I told him to jump up on Frosty's back and I would lead him home.

True to her word Margaret did telephone me and she did call for me once every week for the next year for our lessons, and in that space of time we became firm friends.

We shared many a laugh at the riding school in spite of the very strict teacher, Mr. Carr, but he had a keen sense of humour and I think he thoroughly enjoyed teaching Margaret and I.

Such as the time when he made me put a sixpence between my knees and the saddle. "This exercise is to stop you bobbing up and down in the saddle when you're doing a sitting trot," he said. "You lose that sixpence and I'll charge you double for your lesson, keep it there all through the lesson, and I'll let you off scot-free." His other deterrent for making you sit well-down in the saddle was to place a leaf under your posterior, and threaten you with his long riding whip if it didn't stay there. We never did get a free lesson, but it was always good for a laugh.

Margaret had taken me to the riding school for some weeks, when one afternoon she suddenly said to me.

"Phil, when we've finished the lesson would you like to come home with me for a nice cup of tea?"

"Thank's Margaret," I said. "I'd love to."

On the way there Margaret suddenly stopped the car by the side of the road near a bunch of small bushes, and as she got out of the car, she said, "I won't be a minute Phil, I'm just going to pick some of those leaves."

I wondered what she wanted them for, I hoped she wasn't going to use them to make the tea. Well, there's all kinds of tea!

However, my curiosity was soon satisfied when she returned to the car with her arms full of leafy branches.

"These are for my goats," she said. "They love them."

I raised my eyebrows in surprise. Oh, one lives and learns, I thought. Anyway, I never knew she kept goats, she'd never mentioned them before. However, I was soon to learn a great deal about those creatures that I had yet to meet.

We arrived at her home, which was old, wide and rambling, with about half an acre of lawn, a flower garden, a vegetable patch and a few flowering shrubs, and in the far corner, were some timber-framed, wire-mesh, sheds, which I could see housed the goats.

"That's the young nanny I'm hoping to breed from," she said. "Isn't she sweet? I'm taking her to the Billy Goat soon, would you like to come and lend a hand?"

I should have refused there and then, but ever helpful was I.

So some weeks later, when the nanny came into season, Margaret called me on the telephone.

"Phil," she said, "Can you come over later, if I call for you, I'm going to have the Nanny served"....

Good God! I thought, I don't fancy eating goats meat, whatever excuse can I give her for not going for the meal.

I hesitated for a moment before answering her, then I boldly asked "Why are you killing her?"

"Killing who?" she said.

"Why the little goat of course," I replied. "You said you were serving her."

"Yes I did," she said. "I'm taking her to be served by the Billy, not on a platter — silly."

"Phew! That's a relief," I said, "Yes I'll come, what time will you be wanting me?"

"Oh not today," she said. "I'll come over for you on Friday, about ten o'clock. How's that?"

Friday came round all too quickly, and I still wasn't sure exactly what was expected of me, when Margaret came to call about nine-thirty.

"Aren't you ready yet?" she asked me.

"Sure I am," I replied.

"That's a pretty dress you have on," she said as she eyed me up and down. "But it's hardly suitable for the occasion, we're going to a mating you know ..... not a wedding."

She laughed! "Well not exactly, put some old clothes on like mine."

"Oh well" I said. "If that's what you want I won't argue, it will only take me a minute to go and change."

It was to be the wisest move I ever made.

"OPERATION GOAT ...... HAD ...... BEGUN......"

We went back to Margaret's house first, to collect the little nanny, I thought she sensed there was something amiss, as she seemed so jumpy and nervous.

"How are you transporting her?" I asked.

"By station wagon of course," said Margaret.

"That's if you can get her to go in," I replied.

"Oh she'll go in all right," my friend informed me. "I'll just back the wagon up to the shed, then you can climb in with a bucket of food and some greenery, and when she jumps in, I will slam the door shut, and we'll be ready to roll."

"Oh no! My dear." I said. "If anyone's going into the back with her, it will be you! and when she goes in ... I will slam the door shut, and YOU... can climb back over and into the driver's seat."

"COWARD." shouted Margaret.

After much bleating and kicking, we girls, finally managed to load the struggling nanny into the wagon, but as soon as we took off, she started to fuss....

First she spread the straw all over the wagon, she wet it then tossed it around. Some went on my head, but most of it wrapped itself around Margaret's shoulders and on the steering wheel, where it lodged in a sticky, wet mess.

She laid down, she got up, she rolled over and over, she carried on so that I dared to look round to see if she was doing herself a mischief.

It was then that I noticed a light van, with driver and passenger following in our wake.

The driver was smirking, noticing he had my attention his passenger began to wave and then to fix his hands above his head with his fingers outstretched he made motions, imitating a horned species.

"There's an idiot behind us Margaret." I said. "Don't look back now, but he thinks he's being funny."

I told her what he was doing.

"Serves him right if he had an accident," she said.

But she had to smile all the same. I said to Margaret, "if we don't get to the mating ground soon, one of us might have an accident through laughing." And I didn't mean the car type either.

We found the old farmstead, at the end of a hole-in-the-corner-back lane. My the ground was muddy! So muddy in fact that our vehicle got bogged down just inside the front gate.

I alighted and looked about me and all I could see was GOATS!

They were everywhere, little ones, big ones, black, white, and brown ones. The noise was terrible, and the smell was even worse.

There were some in cage-like structures, and some penned in old disused stables with low-hung doors. And over the open doorway of the last pen of all, was the ugliest goat I had ever seen.

So this was the Billy!

His large, heavy head, great horns and shaggy-bedraggled beard was a frightening sight. So this was the would-be bridegroom!

Margaret was right beside me, clutching the poor half-scared-out-of-her-wits nanny, tightly in her arms.

Jeez! No wonder the nanny was scared. Just seeing let alone mating with a face like that ... would have me screaming and kicking too......

Now I would never have believed that at any time in my life that I would be a party to rape, but a kind of rape it was. And if I live to be ninety, I would never volunteer for that kind of job again.

Margaret and I turned to face each other, and by the look on her face I thought she was going to cancel-out the whole project. She might well have done.

But before she had the chance to turn tail and run, the owner of the goats appeared on the scene.

She was a strikingly large woman, tall, with massive shoulders and arms that showed bulging muscles. Her hair was grey-streaked and tied back into a bun. Her face was weather-beaten as one exposed to wind and sun. Her hands were large and masculine and she dressed that way too.

She wore a pair of men's whip-cord trousers, tucked into high rubber boots, a thick polo-necked sweater and a sleeveless mole-skin jacket. She looked tough! And I for one was glad of the fact, because I could see we were going to need some strong-arm tactics, before the deed was done.

Mrs. Beard, came closer to peer at the nanny.

"Now come along ladies," she said in a deep, gruff voice.

"We haven't got all day! Who is going to help me?"

"I am, Mrs. Beard," I heard Margaret say in a shaky voice.

"Is that really her name?" I asked Margaret as I tried to suppress a chuckle.

"Shush!" Margaret whispered, then she said. "I hope this won't take too long, I'm so hot and sweaty." I could see she was tired and her boots were covered in mud.

Eventually Mrs. Beard came back to us, leading the bridegroom on a piece of strong chain. Actually, he seemed to be leading her, he was so big and strong......

The Billy gave the Nanny a few loving licks, but she wasn't having any of that nonsense, she wasn't at all keen on his loving ministrations; and when he jumped on her back she pulled away in fright dragging poor Margaret with her through the mud.

Up Margaret got and took her back for another try.

The Billy Goat, was beginning to lose his patience!

He made a frantic dive for the luckless nanny as he dashed between Mrs. Beard and me. Then around me he went like a maypole dancer, the long chain from his collar wrapping itself around my knees. Down I went, with the old goat on top of me. Finding no fun with me, he backtracked in the opposite direction, un-tangling my legs. I staggered up, as he made a bee-line for my friend and her protégé.

Margaret fell down, lost the lead rope, then away the nanny flew like a bird on the wing.

Now I've chased some runaway horses and escapee chickens in my time, but trying to catch a sex-crazed goat and his victim in a muddy enclosure, hampered by so many of their four-legged friends, wasn't easy. However, we did catch them.

We tied the rope and the chain-lead together and wound them tightly around the trunk of a nearby tree.

"That should hold them," said Mrs. Beard, in a breathless voice. "Let's get back to the matter in hand."

"Now!" she said to me. "You hold onto her head, and you Mrs. Mells, make sure the leads don't get tangled up, I'll stand at the back and supervise."

Better her than me, I thought. At least, I wasn't near the kicking end.

At last the dastardly deed was done; and as Margaret and I tried to calm the shivering nanny, Mrs. Beard led the satisfied Billy away.

She came back a short time later, after we had put the nanny away.

She poked her head through the window of the wagon and addressed our little friend, thus....

"I don't know what all the fuss was about, you're lucky he took a liking to you."

There was no response...

It was a good thing maybe that the little animal couldn't reply, as the air instead of being just hot and muggy, might have turned ..... blue....

The bride was very quiet on the way home.

The mating however, did turn out very successful.

She did have ..... KIDS.......TWINS......

# Chapter Eleven

# GYMKHANA TIME

It wasn't too long after the Nanny's twins were born, when Bertie said to me....

"How would you like to take another trip to Canada?"

"Oh I can't," I said, "I can't leave Ray again."

"I didn't ask you to," he said.

"You can take him with you this time. How's that?"

"But how are you going to cope?" I asked him.

"Same as last time," he said.

"If you take Ray I'm sure the others can look after themselves, Irene will help."

"It will have to be in September," I said. "I'll be too busy before."

"That's fine," he said. "The fares will be cheaper then."

I had enjoyed the last trip, and I called to mind what Lawrence's sister Doreen has said.

"If you come again I'll take you to Texas with me, we'll take the camper and the trailer, then we can ride the horses for part of the way and use the trailer for the rest of the journey."

I told Bert about Doreen's kind offer.

"Are you mad," he said.

"Do you realize how far it is from Ontario to Texas."

"It would take weeks, even months.... and you'll never stand the pace; besides," he said, "you're walking bandy now, think what you'll be walking like after that long trip."

"Thanks!" I said. "I can do without your wisecracks."

"Anyway," he continued, "don't make too many rash plans, I was only going to suggest that you go for two weeks."

"If you do want to go, I suggest you write to Doreen and explain, don't you?"

So in early September, Ray and I took off.

We had a marvelous time and the weather was great all through the holiday.

*Shirley on Foxy showjumping*

We went to Niagara-on-the-Lake, The Western Fair and we also spent a glorious week in a summer cottage on the shores of Lake Huron. Sad to say I never did get to ride on that trip.

Doreen was told she had cancer, and could never ride again. Ray, not being used to so much sun, was badly sunburned.

My sister-in-law had a baby and my niece got married. And I helped a vet to rescue a cow that was trapped in a small ravine..... Not bad going for two weeks holiday.

When I got home I was in for another surprise.

Anthony and Pat were to be married the second week in October, and boy did I have to get my skates on to get a new outfit for the wedding.

But all this was at the end of the year.

In the merry month of May, Bertie decided to take Smoky to his first horse show. Now that was a very eventful day.

The show was held in Brizes Park on the first Saturday in May, and believe it or not Bertie actually took the day off from work.

Shirley said she would get Cobber ready first then come back to help me with Bridgit.

"We'll go in for the gymkhana events," she said.

"That'll be fun, and perhaps you and Bridgit can enter for the tack and turn-out; you should do alright in that, your tack's always spotless."

"That's not really the problem," I said, "it's the other part that worries me, fancying Bridgit up and trying to keep her that way, and you know she won't let me do her tail."

"Well! Why don't you ask Bert?" she said.

"Oh he won't help me, I replied. "He's too busy getting Smoky ready. He's entering him for the yearling in-hand class. Didn't you know?"

"Oh in that case," she said, "why don't you ask Vic? I'm sure he'll help you." I knew Vic was going to the show, he was entering his gelding, Palladin in the show-jumping.

I'll ask him I thought, he can only say no.

But he didn't. And on the Saturday morning he called to me from across his garden fence.

"I'll be over to help you Phil, as soon as Palladin's ready, okay?"

"Take your brushes over to the stable and I'll join you there soon."

So after I'd cleared the breakfast things and did a quick flick around with the duster I collected my bag of tricks, the dandy brush, curry comb, hoof pick and the rest of the beautifying paraphenalia and made my way over to the stable to join Bridgit. Nessa Mells, Margaret's daughter and Dianne, had already taken Lady Jane and Frosty to the show.

Irene and Bertie were over at the other stables seeing to Smoky.
I was about halfway through cleaning Bridgit, when Vic appeared.
"Boy!" he said, "it's a chilly old morning."
"Yes," I said, "it is pretty cool."
"Not to worry lass," he said, "we'll soon get warm working. And I've
bought along a little drop of cheer, if that don't work.
Well, we brushed and we combed..... and we had a little drink... and
the Mare's coat shone.... Vic, even managed to do her tail.
I said. "She looks perfect."
"What about her legs?" Vic said. "I think they could do with a polish.
Before I could stop him he crawled under and between the Mare's front
legs. It was then I noticed he had a tin of black boot polish in his hand
and before my astonished gaze, he whipped out the boot brush, dipped
it in the polish and gave Bridgit's legs a thorough shoe-shine.
And when he had finished he stuck his head out from between the
mare's legs and said, "What a fine pair of legs you have.... Mam!"
I laughed so much I almost cried.
"Come on Phil," Vic said, "there's a good girl go back to the house make
yourself a cup of coffee and change and I'll lead the old girl ....over.
I went off to get ready. I never thought to glance at the clock. I don't
think I realized how long we had taken to get the mare ready, but when
I did finally get to the show...... my event was all over.....
"Where have you been?" shouted Irene crossly as I trotted over to the
showing enclosure.
"Your event was over long ago," she said.
"Oh my god, what have you done to her legs? and there's black stuff
all over your jodpurs," she screamed.
I only giggled.
"It's not funny," she said, "but now you're here, you can go over and
help Dad with Smoky.
"Do I have to?" I said. I still felt a bit drowsy.
"Yes!" she hollered, "he's just over there by the refreshment tent."
I trotted over to where they stood and dismounted, Smoky seemed
jumpy so I patted him on the rump and said, "Hello! Smoky! you look
very handsome." And I gave him a hug for luck. Bridgit whinnied and
pushed close to him.
"Get her out of the way," said Bertie, crossly.
"How can I keep him under control with her stuck there?"
"That's nice," I said, "after I've come over to help you."

"The best way you can help," he said, "is to get that Cart-Horse out of the way."

I was hurt, but I guessed he must have been having some kind of trouble, so I excused his temper that time.

I walked over to the refreshment tent leading Bridgit. I went to the counter.

Someone must have ordered a plate of sandwiches then walked away for something. I turned around to see who it could be, and as soon as my back was turned, Bridgit had quietly edged forward and without a sound demolished them all and slurped the two cups of tea that stood beside them.

I pulled her away as quickly as I could. She was furious. She tossed her head and pulled on the reins to get back probably hoping for more. I gave her a tap with the riding crop and we made a speedy retreat to the in-hand show ring, and there I saw Smoky and his master. Ha! Ha!

It was Smoky doing the leading or should I say dragging for Bertie, who was no light weight, was being pulled around the ring as if he were a paper-doll. My spouse wasn't very pleased I could see, and I don't think the judges were very impressed either..... so I wasn't surprised when he wasn't even placed.

I thought, that will be his last time in the ring.

How right I was......

Frosty and Lady won first and second place in their show-jumping class, and Frosty with Shirley won the challenge cup for the 14 hand; and that same afternoon I met my soon-to-be daughter-in-law's Mother.

She had gone to the show with Pat and Anthony, no doubt to have an enjoyable afternoon.

How was I to know it was she who had ordered those sandwiches and tea, and, she had seen the two culprits....

However, I made up for her lost luncheon when she came back to my house after the show. And later that evening we took her and her husband over to our favorite Pub to meet some of our friends.

Andrew enjoyed a game of darts with the Metson lads, and Alice, Pat's mum, related the tale of the missing tea and sandwiches to an amused audience.

Alice was a real sport, but when I asked her if she would like to learn to ride, she said, "I've tried many things, but I'll never try that. Who knows, if the horse gets hungry, she might eat me."

And there was certainly a lot of Alice.......

# Chapter Twelve

# OUR FARMER FRIENDS

Although I spent a great deal of my time with my family and the horses, I did find the time to make many friends, and the most treasured of all were the Metson's.

There was George and his wife Hilda, their three sons and their wives and George's numerous grandchildren.

The Metson's, were a close-knit family and most of the land around Roxwell where they lived had been farmed by their forefathers for many generations, and the family being so large they would very likely continue to do so for many more years to come.

George was semi-retired when we first got to know him, he did help out occasionally on the farm, and he also tended a fine vegetable garden; but his chief interest was the raising of free-range chickens and selling their eggs. Come Christmas time he sold prime turkeys.

The eggs he sold were delicious and we managed to get through three trays a week, the rest we sold at the store.

So, on Thursday afternoons when Bertie and I went to the tiny village of Ongar for our weekly groceries, we would visit the Metson's to collect the eggs.

Now there was a quaint little village. The villagers did say, that its fine parade of shops dated back to the seventeenth century, when shops such as these had a certain air of genteel tranquility. Most of the buildings were tall and narrow in shape with small latticed windows that hardly let in any light at all, making it rather difficult for short-sighted persons such as myself to distinguish the goods for sale within.

Other buildings appeared to be slightly crooked and lean drunkenly towards their neighbours. Maybe the workmen in the Tudor era had been in the Old Lion and Lamb Inn before commencing their labours. Some of the shops were higher than the pavement itself and were made accessible by a flight of well-worn steps leading up into their dark interior. Others were entered by steps leading down from the shop's doorway, and once the door was opened a brass bell would let forth a merry jangle, probably to keep alert any would-be sleepy assistant that had ideas of dropping off for forty winks in the middle of the day.

Nestling between The Tudor and Elizabethan establishments was to be found the old Quaker Hall and a few Alms houses and at the beginning of the High Street was the oldest pub of all; The Two Brewers. This Inn was built on an angle by the side of the River Roding and there, all through the summer months the local lads could be seen doing a spot of fishing.

A much nicer occupation than shopping any day.

To the right of the bridge was the Green Line Country Bus stop. I liked that idea, because while you were waiting for the bus it was pleasant to watch the anglers.

Going back to the High Street and its shops, all of them full of such interesting wares, I was always intrigued with the Pharmacist. On most of my shopping expeditions I was always amused to see a large Tabby Tom Cat sunning himself in the large bay window amidst the cosmetics and the perfumery, quite oblivious to the passers by. In the other bay window, centrally placed was a set of three green bottles, known in the trade as Apothecary Jars.

These large flagon-shaped bottles were the olden day symbols of the herbalist, unique and a collectors item I was sure.

To continue up the street along the left-hand side, halfway between the butchers and the bank was a well-frequented Inn where an old man in a white cap and apron sold shellfish from a stall set up in the Inn's cobblestoned yard.

You could hear his cries — way off ...

"Cockles! Fine Cockles! Fresh from Lea today. What about a fine lobster lady? or a crab? So fresh, they'll wink at y'er." And just behind his stall a carpet trader could be heard plying his wares.

"Carpets! Lovely Carpets! Come and look 'em over Missus, there's no charge for looking."

And if he grew thirsty from shouting, there was always the Lion and Lamb Inn — to go in for a pint of the very best ale.

However, there was a drawback to shopping in this village as the narrowness of the High Street pavement posed a problem, as more often than not the customers would have to duck and dive between tradesmen's vans being unloaded before they could gain access to the shop, and sidestepping on the pavement was courting disaster, one slight accidental push and you could find yourself in the road.... or worse. The stream of traffic passing through this village was constant, as the High Street was the main thorough-fare between the City of London, and the Harwich Docks.

All day, and far into the night, large continental six-wheel trucks drove through, shaking the old dwellings to their very foundations. At any minute you expected one of them to come tumbling down about your ears, and as those monstrous trucks went by, passing pedestrians would have to flatten themselves against the shaking walls; and trying to cross the road at peak shopping hours, was like trying to commit suicide. But what annoyed me the most was the two stupidly placed pedestrian crossings, that to my way of thinking, were placed too far apart, one of them should have been in the centre of the street, instead of one at each end. This state of affairs proved an extreme aggravation to me, especially when I wanted to go from the butchers to the Co-operative grocery stores across the road; where I could buy Wines, Spirits, Clothing, Yarn and Drapery.

There was also a news-vendor who also sold cigarettes and candy. A florist, a toy shop and a jewelry store.

At the far end of the shopping parade was the Post Office, a Bank, two coffee shops and the Budworth Hall. This hall was used for weddings, bingo, and as the committee rooms at election time. Next to Budworth Hall were two parking lots and, if you could spare the time or had enough patience to wait for a vacant spot, that was fine, otherwise you took your chances by parking in front of the stores, wedged between a bus or a large biscuit van, hoping that the delivery to the store wouldn't take too long or you might be wedged in there for the rest of the day.

This Thursday's shopping was a hazardous affair, but we had to eat. So after all the hassle I was glad when Bertie said to me.

"Never mind Phil, now that's all over we can nip over to George's for a nice cup of tea."

When we arrived, Hilda would put the kettle on and out would come some of her homemade cakes and tarts.

"Sit yourself down me dear," she would say, "while I brew the tea."

"Come on in here Bert and sit along of George, I got a nice piece of cake 'ere for you."

During the tea, George and Bert would talk about the weather, the price of hay and eggs, and how they would put the world to rights. While Hilda and I would discuss the Women's Institute, recipes and the families. Later the men would tour the vegetable garden, the farmyard, and the henhouse, while Hilda and I would go next door to her sons to see SUGAR and SPICE....their two ponies.

Later that evening we would once again wend our way to the Metson's and go with them to their local pub, where we would gather in a circle in the saloon bar to have a drink, swap stories and have a good gossip, sometimes we would join the menfolk in a friendly game of darts. Well, it was friendly while they were winning.

This pub in the field was once owned by Hilda's parents, the locals called it the Cuckoo! Its rightful name was The Thatchers Arms. This one time wayside Inn stood in the middle of a one-acre field at the end of a long, winding lane, a privet hedge dividing the field from the concrete path that led to the pub's entrance. The gravelled left-hand space was used as a car park, the right-hand side half acre of grassy meadowland was for the tethering of well-mannered horses and ponies, tethered at the owner's risk and at the Landlord's pleasure. Although he grumbled sometimes it really pleased him to have them there as they served as an added attraction to his business. I made full use of this spot for many years. There and back, it was only a sixteen mile hack from my front door. It was a good hack and I always enjoyed my lunch there, a glass of cider and a cheese or ham sandwich.

The ride was exhilarating, especially the gallops across the stubble fields in September and the long treks through the Co-op farms empty fields. To feel the wind blowing through my hair and the excitement coursing through my veins as I galloped out on Frosty in the crisp morning air of early October.

It was sheer heaven going to and fro from that village pub and I always reckoned it could tell a tale or two from the days of yore when ghostly riders roamed the flat Essex marshlands, to meet up with smugglers from the beaches along the east coast. When highwaymen, like Dick Turpin and John Smith would lie in wait at the side of the road for the unwary coach travellers to appear over the horizon. Probably archery contests and old time hunt meets would have happened on this very spot that I had ridden over so many times.

There would be tales to tell, maybe from the Viking days, for this part of the country was steeped in history, but whatever had taken place here in the past belonged to another era; and if the outside structure hadn't altered very much, the prices certainly had. For in a far corner of the public bar by the window was a penned map of the Essex countryside and a faded parchment in old worlde script of the prices for fare, board and lodging; and underneath on a scroll was a list of rules for the boarders, and how to control wayward horses.

So even in those days they had troublesome horses.

And we owned some, as the Metson's well knew.

Take Cobber, for example he was a horse with few vices apart from the wanderlust, he was good on the road and easy to shoe but he always had to be the big boss, and always at feeding time, when he had to taste every bucket full first.

The mares were scared of him, but not so Frosty and Speedy, that was another story. Usually ending with a kick-up and a vet's bill, so Irene and I came up with a solution.

It was simple really, we persuaded Bertie to fix another gate halfway down the field. At feeding time, Irene would dash down to the centre gate with three buckets and I would stand at the ready at the end gate with mine. At a given signal she would climb over her gate with the mare's and Speedy's food and I would squeeze between the end gate's rails with Frosty's and Cobber's.

I was lucky not to have my rear end bitten off in the affray.

I would dearly loved to have known how they knew when it was suppertime, did they have pocket watches hidden away?

Once they started to eat was the time to stand well clear for I knew how dangerous it could be to stand between a horse and his food, or near two horses eating too close together.

Ears back was the first signs of hostility, and as Bertie used to say, and I sincerely believed him. "Never go behind their back legs, never! Unless you talk to them first and stroke their rump, or you'll get a swift kick where it hurts." He also told me. "There was no such thing as a too friendly critter."

"You remember young Micky?" He said, "when his Shetland Pony picked him up by his sweater, shook him hard and then bit him?"

"Yes I do!" I answered him.

"Right," he said. "You get a nasty animal and they can be a killer. And what I hate to see," he continued "is some fool of a mother letting her small child ride out on a pony ... alone. And another thing," he said "don't let me catch you taking a horse out just before you feed him, he'll throw you off for sure, and he'll come back without you."

He was always having a go at me but I did learn quite a lot about horses from him. Some things I noticed myself.

Such as; taking a different route whilst out hacking, the mount I rode would seem to slow his pace, turn his head from side to side, and if that mount could have spoken I'm sure the conversation would have sounded something like this,

"Hi! where do you think you're taking me? I've never been this way before."

I'm sure they could sense bad weather approaching, as at the slightest hint of high winds or a clap of thunder, it was hard not to stop them from turning about and galloping back to home base.

Horses were troublesome too, when you tried to groom them in the fields, when the blackberries were ripe and to tie one to a nearby bush was courting disaster and it wasn't too clever either to pick the fruit while they were around.

Bridgit would follow you, trying to push her nose into the bucket and if you ignored her wants, she would give you a playful push and send you head first into the prickly bushes. Painful...

I must admit I enjoyed the life attending to horses, although sometimes I was sorely tried and completely lost my temper.

Especially on wet wintry days, when the wind blew like mad across the Essex marshes and the ground of soft clay became so muddy it sucked at my boots.

Why was it at this time that the manure pile in the stables always seemed bigger, and the carting of it to the pile grew more hazardous every day. The times that I screamed when the wheelbarrow that had almost reached the top of the pile, tilted, collapsed and turned over as the wooden ramp I was manoeuvering it on broke under the strain, causing me to go down with it into the muck and mire.

However, more surprises and harder graft was yet to come.

# Chapter Thirteen

# A HORSE'S BRUSH WITH THE LAW

In the February of nineteen-seventy-three, Irene decided that she would like to buy and raise a young Filly of her very own. She had scrutinized the "For Sale" pages of the "Horse and Hounds" magazine for some months: and was very interested in the advertisement in the "Spring Issue".

FOR SALE
YOUNG THOROUGHBRED FILLY
MAKE 15 .2
DARK BAY — UNBROKEN
CALL OR WRITE.

The Filly it said, was at stables in a country village in Norfolk, A County on the East Coast.

Irene rang the owners, and they promised to bring the Filly along the following Saturday afternoon.

Now that was a journey of just under a hundred miles, and the young people who delivered her arrived at our house very late at night, so late in fact, that we had almost given them up for lost.

The young Filly was tired and hungry. So while Bert and I discussed the details of the sale, Irene took the little mare over to the vacant isolated stable; bedded her down and gave her some water and hay.

We always isolated a new arrival until they were cleared by the vet. It was safer that way, and prevented any trouble later on.

The filly's papers were in order and after a bit of haggling we agreed upon a price. Then Irene and the owners made an agreement. We were to board the filly for two weeks, on approval, and if we were dissatisfied in any way we were told to phone the stables and they would make arrangements to come and collect her on the Sunday morning of the second week.

I made them some supper and listened as they told us the difficult time they had finding our home.

"We missed the turn off," they said, "and we drove all the way to Brentwood first before we discovered our mistake."

"Would you like to stay the night?" I asked them.

"No! sorry," they said, "but we have a show fixed for tomorrow: so, we'll just finish our tea and be on our way."

On Monday morning I phoned the vet, explained about the new mare and asked if he could come over to see her.

He said he couldn't come until Tuesday.

"I'll try to make it about nine o'clock," he said.

Tuesday morning around eight-thirty, he was on my doorstep.

"Hello! not out riding yet I see," he said, giving me a saucy grin.

"I don't spend all day riding, you know," I answered him. "I have other chores to do."

"Such as helping me," he said with a chuckle. "Now you know you've always got time for that."

"It looks like I'll have to," I said. "For a very long time,"

"Where's the newcomer you want me to examine?" he asked.

"Why! she's over there in the stable yonder, hang on a moment and I'll take you over there."

"Ah! you have got a nice little lass here," he said, as he examined the filly: "She's a real beauty and no mistake."

"What's her name?" he asked.

"Foxy Lady," I told him.

"When you've finished examining her, perhaps you would like to come back to the house and see her papers; and while you're there you might just as well join me in a cup of tea."

I allowed him to study the mare's papers, then I told him where she came from.

"Oh yes," he said, "I've heard of those breeders, they do say that they run a very efficient and reputable establishment."

"What do you think of her?" I asked.

"Oh! she's in fine shape. And I should certainly keep her if I were you."

"She's not mine," I said, "she belongs to my daughter."

"Well you tell her from me, she has a real bargain there, she will never make a race horse, but she will make a fine Lady's hunter."

When Irene came home from work that evening, I told her all that the vet had said. She was over the moon, and before she had any supper she dashed over to the stable to see the little mare.

Thursday afternoon I rode Frosty up from the big fields and lodged him in the stable next to hers.

There was a fair bit of whinnying for awhile but they soon settled down, but I did wonder what was going to happen when they were let out to graze together.

I could see the pair of them quite clearly from the kitchen window which was most convenient for me, as was the feed store which was attached to the end stable.

So there enthroned, was another mouth to feed, and another mucky stable to clean out.

"Oh well! with three pairs of willing hands the extra chore didn't seem too bad.

But there was more.... to come.

It was really a rather sad day when El Tonto came to us. His owner, a young lady from nearby Brentwood, phoned me one evening to enquire if we would like to buy her gelding.

The price was low, and she explained why. She said, "I think he's blind in one eye."

"Oh! how sad," I said. "Are you sure?"

"Well, he appears to be," she said, "although I haven't actually consulted a vet."

She paused, and I thought I detected a trace of a sob in her voice.

"Are you still there?" I asked.

After a few minutes the voice continued, only this time I knew the person on the other end of the line was crying.

"Yes," she sobbed, then paused again.

"I'm sorry, please forgive me," she said.

"I really don't want to part with my horse: but, I've just been told by my doctor that I have cancer, and I'll never be able to ride again."

Oh my God, I thought, poor thing, as my memory was awakened by sad thoughts of my friend, Doreen.

More horses, more stable cleaning, more chores: the vivid picture arrayed itself before my eyes: but I couldn't say no when her pleading voice asked me.

"Will you take him..... please?"

"Sure I'll take him," I said, without giving a thought as to what my spouse would say.

"You'll have to give me a few days," I told her gently, "until I sort something out as to where I am going to stable him. Can you leave me your phone number, and I'll call you back as soon as I've spoken to my husband? He's out playing darts at the moment."

I waited until I heard how Bertie had fared in the darts match before I delivered my bombshell.

But I needn't have worried, he was just as soft-hearted as me.

"If you want him," he said, "it's okay by me, but, you will have to find a spare stable to rent and an extra piece of grazing land, until El Tonto, is cleared by the vet."

"Where did he get that handle?" I said. "I hope he understands English, or I shall have to take Spanish lessons before he arrives."

The following week I was rushed off my feet: and I ran up a large phone bill as I frantically phoned and searched around the neighbourhood seeking quarters for the newly acquired addition to our ever increasing flock.

By the end of that week I had acquired a stable and a small storage shed from the publican of the Eagle, just a quarter-mile away, on the main Brentwood to Ongar Highway.

The extra grazing land was across the road from the stable, it was a small field, situated next to the village police station.

Tall trees and a high hedge protected the enclosure on three sides: the entrance from the road was through a wooden five-bar gate, padlocked and tied firmly with binder twine, to keep our four-legged friends in ... and unwanted visitors out.

The trees offered shade aplenty in Summer and acted as a windbreak in Winter. A large iron trough for water stood by the side of the gate: the water had to be carried by the bucketful from Shirley's house, one hundred yards from the field — water for the stable, likewise.

Ponies drank a great deal of water. How much would this fellah drink? I asked myself.

Our first meeting was mutually friendly. He nuzzled my hand to lick the salt after expecting a polo-peppermint.

He was seventeen hands, rangy with narrow shoulders, and very high on the withers, but in poor shape — his ribs protruded from either side of his rib-cage, he was quite docile-looking for his size.

I was pleased when the vet gave him the once-over.

"Ah! What this poor lad needs is some good fodder inside him and he'll soon shape up, you wait and see. I can't see anything drastically wrong with his eye that care and a little medication won't put right. People that put horses in this condition should be shot! Give me a call in two weeks time if you have any further problems."

As there were no complications and no contagious illness diagnosed, we agreed to allow Bridgit to keep El Tonto company, we had been assured that he was bombproof on the highway — that is to say, it was safe to take him out hacking on very busy roads.

We were hoping his actions would serve to allay Bridgit's fears of the heavier traffic. They became the best of stablemates.

We now had three sets of horses in three different places: two beside the Eagle, two stabled in the field behind the house, and three others down in the big main fields in Doddinghurst, two miles from home base.

We had recently sold Speedy: Ray, had outgrown him.

Once these arrangements had been sorted out, Bert and Irene suddenly sprung on me news about their intended visit to Canada that same summer.

"For goodness sake." I said to them, "How am I going to cope for three weeks on my own! You know I can't drive!"

"Oh, you'll have plenty of help: there's Shirley and her Dad, and Dianne — the horses won't be any trouble."

Ha! Ha! Famous last words — how wrong they turned out to be.

My husband and I never holidayed together: because of our many commitments, one of us had to stay home.

There was a business to run as well as a family and animals to be taken care of.

Family can't be left too long by themselves either, whether they be two or twenty. They may raid the freezer, entertain their friends by eating you out of house and home, not to mention using up jars and jars of coffee, playing the radio too loudly, and turning your home into a hotel. No, holidays had to be taken separately.

Everything went according to plan during the first week after I took over the reins. Friends were helpful and the weather remained fine, which made the hard chore of mucking-out much easier. Even my laundry chores were soon finished leaving me more time for my extra duties. Things went so smoothly that I had the feeling that it was all too good to be true. Certainly it was too good to last. How right I was.

On the Saturday morning bright and early, before the dawn chorus, I heard a great deal of noise coming from the direction of the home stables, and as I looked out of the bedroom window I thought I saw two shapes messing about by the food store.

I said to myself, "Now what's wrong?"

I dashed downstairs and through to the kitchen and picking up my spectacles I ran over to the kitchen window and there I saw the two horses. They were out of their stalls and rummaging about by the open door of the feed-store.

"Good grief," I said as I made a grab for Geoff's duffle coat that was left as usual on the back of the kitchen chair, and his old running shoes which I hastily slipped on my feet.

Still mumbling and carrying on by saying a few choice angry words about horses in general, I dashed out of the back door, grabbed a spare piece of washing-line from a hook on the wall, and sprinted like an athlete across the dewy-wet grass to the field entrance gate at the bottom of the garden. Losing one shoe in the process, I hopped back for it, losing precious seconds: and more time was lost as my hands that were all fingers and thumbs struggled to untie the knot in the string around the top of the gate.

I finally succeeded, and I could hear myself shouting as I ran, "You nasty pair of horrors, wait until I get hold of you," I brandished my arms like one demented as I ran across the field to the food store — and the couldn't-care-less truants — standing there.

A sorry sight met my eyes!...... Those two terrors, Frosty and Foxy Lady, who must have been out of their stalls for hours, had their heads deeply entrenched in two upturned food bins, guzzling away to their hearts content.

"Oh my God!" I shouted to the empty space devoid of all human life at that time in the morning.

"How on earth did you manage to get in there?"

As if they would have told me — even if they could.

By then they had demolished a whole bin of oats, and half a bag of sugar beet, not to mention the waste that was scattered about the area of the feed store.

Maybe you've heard the expression or stories — of what happens to folks who've had too may oats? — Yes — With horses it's more serious, they get colic.

So, I had to get them back quickly into their respective stalls far away from any more foodstuff and fix the foodstore door that was hanging from its hinges.

I'd never had the chance to find the halters to lead them in by, so I had to make do with the piece of laundry line and some binder-twine which came from the empty sugar beet sack.

It was too late to summon help — they would have attacked another bin had I turned my back again, even to breathe.

To say how long it took me to return those terrible two would have been an educated guess. But return them I did, single handedly. Then I went back to the house to wake my two sleeping sons. I promised them a breakfast fit for a king if they would get up and go walk-about with those two greedy animals.

"Do we have to," they said.

"Yes you do," I yelled at them, unless you want me up all day and night with them if they get colic." And as an afterthought I said, "And you know what that means? You'll have to do all the other jobs yourselves." That did the trick, they were out of bed like a shot and into the field in double-quick time.

They walked the horses while I cleaned up the store shed and stables, and salvaged what I could of the spilled food.

"Now don't tell your father," I said "I'll have to make good the loss somehow. I don't think I left the door to the shed unlocked."

"Oh go on Mum, you'll be saying the horses unlocked it next."

The next week passed uneventfully. I rode out on El Tonto a few times with Shirley on Cobber. Bridgit made a fuss when we left her alone in the field, but a few carrots and an apple soon appeased her.... food always did.

I can't say I really enjoyed riding El Tonto, his gait wasn't as smooth as Frosty's or Bridgit's, and it seemed a heck of a way up sitting astride him. There was one consolation however, the traffic never seemed to worry him whatever the vehicle, bus or tractor, and even when a motorist slowing down beside him brushed his offside leg, he never even flinched.

I felt confident: but when Shirley said, "shall we go through Coppice Wood?" I said, "Not today, as I feel as tall as the trees that I will have to duck under, and I don't want to leave my head among the top branches."

"Shirley laughed. "I don't think you'll come to any harm," she assured me, "you've always got Dad and me to help out if you get stuck-up somewhere during the next week."

"It'll be nice when Uncle Bert and Irene get back, won't it?" she said.

"It won't be long now," I told her "they've only got another week and I can't see me having any more trouble like the last lot."

"You won't say anything to them about it, will you?"

"Of course I won't," she said, "but if anything like that happens again you will phone me?"

It didn't, at least not until the August Bank Holiday.

The August Bank Holiday started on the Saturday. There were no shows to go to, and the horses were all out grazing, so I thought I would have a nice quiet weekend and put my feet up and maybe write a letter or two.

But.....

Let us go back to the happy-traffic-watching pair of horses in the Kelvedon Field.

Bridgit may have gained a little road sense from El Tonto, but he was not the one who influenced her actions on that afternoon when the constable in residence (with his pretty, young sociable wife and a son of tender years) had cordially invited his father-in-law to stay with them for the holiday weekend in the cottage-cum-police station of Kelvedon Green.

Like most healthy retired seniors, this gentleman enjoyed gardening, and in the warmth of the Saturday afternoon sunshine the keen tiller of the soil was busily weeding the front flower beds of the cottage, which was adjacent to the grazing field.

With no one around to groom or otherwise bother them, the horses had focused their undivided attention on the labouring neighbour on the other side of the high hedge, a nice occupation for both parties. The gardener was in no way perturbed.

In fact, as he told me later, he looked up once or twice to pass a friendly remark to his audience.

However, it was thirsty work, and not just for the gardener.

At four o'clock I quit my letter writing and took a walk through Swan Lane, intending to fill the water trough, and check on the horses at the same time, and I thought, if Shirley's mother was at home, perhaps I might get invited in for a cup of tea or a cold drink. It would be thirsty work filling up the trough. But as I reached the gate of the Old Forge Cottage, I saw my old friend Arthur Mills hard at work mowing his front lawn.

"Hi! Arthur." I called. "I see you're very busy."

Arthur stopped his lawn mower and came over towards me to lean on his garden gate.

"Hello Phil, how are you today? And where do you think you're off to? How's Bert and Irene? Have you heard from them yet? Lucky old devil, I bet he's having the time of his life over there. I'd like to be behind him, see what he's getting up to."

He changed his position by the gate, and his old bitch Bess, a large grey muzzled black labrador, waddled down the garden path to sit at his heels. She was panting and puffing like a steam engine.

"You silly girl," I said affectionately, leaning over the gate to pat her on the head.

"Why don't you find a cool place to sit? By the state you're in it looks like you've been in a hundred yards race."

Arthur looked down at her reprovingly.

"The silly old fool's been chasing rabbits all morning in the fields up at Outings Lane. I told her she was too old and fat for that caper — she'll learn."

"By the way Phil, I spotted young Smoky while I was up there, he was running around alongside Cobber. My he's grown a size, I hardly recognized him, bit different from the last time I saw him, remember? He was so wobbly at the knees that he had a job to stand up to reach his dam's teats. He was a lovable little fellah and no mistake."

"Yes! he's certainly grown." I said. "He'll probably make seventeen hands."

"Speaking of rangy horses," I said. "Have you seen our new addition to the fold?"

"Crikey Yes!" he said. "He's a big'n, what's Bert going to do with him?"

"I don't know," I told him. "We'll have to wait and see when Bert gets back, he's only got another week."

"Good," Arthur said. "Only we've got a darts match coming up in two weeks time, against the Cuckoo. I hope he's been practicing."

"Sure," I said, "I expect he's been using bows and arrows over there." Arthur laughed!

I'm sorry Arthur," I said, "but I have to go now, the'll be two thirsty horses waiting for me around the corner. I'll maybe see you later in the "Shepherd". You can buy me a drink."

I hurried on through the lane, I thought I'd better not stop to talk to anyone else or I'd never get the water trough filled — before dark.

I reached the Ongar Road, turned right, crossed the Eagle Lane walking past the high-privet hedge in front of the police-station on my way to the grazing-field gate.

I was just about to open it when I noticed an elderly man come out of the police-station's front door. He was carrying a bucket of water in one hand and a large glass tankard of (what I thought could be beer) in the other.

He had only taken a few steps along the garden path, when, the action that followed was like a scene from the Circus.

All I saw was a black, heavy-weight of horseflesh flying through the air, not just over the hedge; but also clearing a mini-car that was parked in the driveway.

It was Bridgit! Not to be outdone — El Tonto followed — and all for a bucket of water.

After I recovered from the shock of seeing Bridgit actually jumping; and at a stand too, I ran back to the cottage, threw open the gate, grabbed hold of the mare by the head collar, and hung on like grim death. I never did see what happened to the gardener!

Just then the village Bobby, who must have heard the commotion going on in his front yard dashed out of the cottage in his shirt sleeves, his face covered in shaving foam.

"What the B... Hell's going on out here?" he shouted, "Can't a man have a shave in peace?"

I never answered, I was too busy, trying to catch El Tonto.

It didn't take the constable too long however, to size up the situation. He shoved me aside and nearly pushed me over in his attempt to pass me in order to capture El Tonto, who, at that moment was immobile as his mouth and nostrils were firmly entrenched in the empty water bucket which rattled and clanged noisily as it rolled from side to side on the gravelled driveway. The angry policeman, seizing his opportunity grabbed El Tonto's head collar and held on fast.

We both stood there, panting, the constable, his face brick-red from temper and streaked red and white like a barber's pole from the running soapy lather, made me want to burst-out laughing.

I looked away quickly, turned Bridgit around and was just about to make a speedy exit when a further shout from the law rooted me to the spot.

"For heaven's sake, look at the holes in my lawn," he spluttered. "And just look at my flowerbeds." Then he said a few more choice words that I pretended not to hear. He then proceeded to give me a lecture, about people who left their horses too long with nothing to do. Which made my ears sting for the rest of the day. Red and shame-faced I apologised, but he took no notice.,

"Hurry up and get those damn animals out of here," was all he said.

It was then I think, that the policeman suddenly remembered the unintentional perpetrator of the afternoon's escapade, and we both looked around to see where he could be.

Poor old soul, we found him cringing up against a prickly rose bush — he must have been in a bad way.

"Can I do anything for you?" I said helpfully.

"Don't you think you've done enough," said the officer of the law. "I'll do all the helping!"

And as I walked out of the gate leading Bridgit with El Tonto following I heard him say to the victim.

"Come over here, Dad, come and sit on this bench and I'll go in and get you a stiff drink of whisky."

After I filled the water tank and made sure the horses were settled for the night, I couldn't resist going back to the cottage to find out how the old gentleman was.

"Is it okay if I come in for a moment?" I asked him. He beckoned me in, and as I drew nearer I could see he was still shaky.

Just then the constable came out of his cottage to join us.

"You back again?" he said.

"I've come back to see if your Dad would like me to call a doctor."

"Its not a doctor that's wanted, and you can thank your lucky stars that it's not a mechanic we'll be wanting either. Thank goodness the mini's okay."

"Yes! I'm perfectly okay," the old gentleman informed me as he gave me a knowing wink; I could see, that his hands had grown somewhat steadier as he sipped on a large glass of whisky.

I left the scene of the crime, but before actually departing — and to save face and keep on the right side of the law, I promised to seek out a more desolate spot for the culprits to graze in. Maybe I acted too hastily in finding pastures new.

I was truly sorry afterwards for doing so.

Soon after we vacated that field it took its tragic toll! A young life. The policeman's son went missing; he was found a few days later — drowned — while playing in the empty field, he fell into an open cesspool. It gave us all the shivers every time we passed that field.

As for El Tonto, he didn't remain with us for very long after that unhappy episode. I found looking after him too demanding.

So while my husband was still abroad, I put him up for sale. El Tonto I mean, not my husband.

The gelding went to a good home, his new owner a tall, heavy-set man, a farmer, who said he wanted him for fox-hunting. They made a handsome pair.

I had no regrets as they drove away, but I remembered that horse for a long time, although I had only ridden him a few times.

True, he was well mannered and easy to groom, but he was by far too big a mount for me.

Bert was quite angry when he came home and found out I'd sold him, he called me a horse thief. He said, and I quote.

"Where I come from — you could be strung-up for less." Was I a rustler, or just fed up with too much mucking-out?

Just before Irene went on holiday, we thought we would have a little get together to wish her Bon Voyage! Laurence bought along his girl friend Maraylin, (affectionately known as Maggie) to the party, she asked if she could bring her brother Brian, as she explained, he was anxious to meet us all.

"Sure, the more the merrier," we told her.

The party was a swinging success and before the Canadian trip had started, Irene and Brian were seeing quite a lot of each other, so much so that as the time to leave drew near, Irene was reluctant to go; and after the food-bin raiding episode I wished she hadn't gone; and I was jolly glad when she came back.

They said they had a marvellous time, visiting all the places of Bertie's youth, the old school house and the stream where he used to go fishing and the various farms he worked on. They also went to Niagara to see the Falls and the big city of Toronto. And they spent a week in the same cottage on Lake Huron, where Ray and I had enjoyed such a wonderful time together. However, they never did get to ride any horses ... But I don't think that worried Irene too much.

To her, there were no other horses to equal our own and she said she was glad to get back to them.

A few weeks after the holiday makers return, Lady Jane cut her leg on a bottle that some lazy person had thrown in the field, so I had to call the vet.

After he had finished stitching up the wound, I asked him when he would come over again, as we wanted him to geld Smoky.

"He's getting to frisky," I said, "and out of hand, and if he is to stay in the field with the others I think he should be done quite soon."

"I know what you mean," he said, "I'll try and make it next week if I can, I'll get my secretary to phone you."

"Yes please," I said. "Give me plenty of warning, Bert's not wriggling out of his one, I'm definitely not helping you for that job."

Smoky gelded, peace reigned once more in the fields at Blackmore, except of course for escapee Cobber, who did his disappearing trick whenever he got bored. One sunny afternoon he was found sunbathing in the middle of the road in Outings Lane, just outside the doctor's office. The Doctor never came out to minister to his needs, just the boys in blue, from the Blackmore Police Station this time. They called Shirley to collect him and for his punishment he was banished to the Milkman's stables for a week. The next time he went walkabout he took Bridgit and Lady with him, and at four o'clock that same afternoon the three of them were to be seen returning back to base walking very slowly, one behind the other in crocodile fashion as a file of school children, reluctant to return to school. And no matter how many times we fixed the fence he always found an opening, and we always knew where it was as he left a tuft of gingery mane near the escape hole.

The middle of September the horses had to take a back seat for awhile as the family planned and attended Maggie and Laurence's wedding. It was a pretty affair, the coupled looked so young it made me want to cry; however, I never had long to recuperate from that excitement as later in the year, Patricia and Anthony were blessed with identical twin girls. Nicholia and Debra.

That was October — where had the summer gone?

Winter and Christmas had yet to come.

I did remember that year's anniversary, the fifth of November, which coincided with Guy Fawkes Day, when two extremely cold gentlemen, Bertie and Victor, braved the wintry night's elements to sit on upturned straw-bales in the stable, just in case a stray fire-work should alight on the barn's roof, and probably wondering if they had enough beer with them to put the fire out.

I also remember the bitter cold winds, the snow squalls we had that winter. The house parties we attended and the host of new friends that we made. And as Christmas drew near, I began to take note of the extra toys that would be needed for the grandchildren and I tried to remember what each child had asked Santa to bring.

The past year had brought joy and some sorrows, and as I sat by the fire New Year's Eve seeing out the old year and welcoming in the new, I wondered what else life had in store for me; never dreaming for one moment just how sad it was really going to be.

# Chapter Fourteen

# SAD TIDINGS

February, Nineteen-seventy-four, was a tragic month for myself and my family.

It all started with Smoky ...

He had been out to graze in the bottom field at Doddinghurst for over a year, and Irene and her father were breaking him in gently. He was quick to learn and very willing, and in some respects, he was very much like his dam.

Only easy to catch when he thought you had something for him, like food. His favourite nibble was pony nuts. Once bridled, he would walk, trot and canter in circles on command. To get him used to the feel of a saddle, Bert made-up a kind of Dumb-Jockey, by filling a sugar-beet sack with wet straw, weighted down with foam padding. He set it upon Smoky's back.

He didn't like it at first, but he soon got used to it.

He was a lively lad! Always on the trot, either with Lady Jane by his side, or his dam, who recently joined him.

Cobber! he stood clear of ...

He was never any bother, he never tried to play truant like the others, so sometimes we left him to his own devices.

One evening, when all the other horses dashed down to the gates to be fed, Smoky hung back. I wasn't there at the time, but, as Bertie told me later, he wasn't unduly worried at the time as he thought Smoky held back because of Cobber. Probably waiting until the Cob moved off. But when he went back to the fields later that night to collect the empty buckets, taking Irene with him, he said he was surprised to see Smoky standing in the same spot. So, he said, he went over to investigate. He said he called to him. "Smoky! Smoky! Old fellah! Come on! Come on! Don't you want your food?"

"I watched him," Bert continued, "I saw him put his head up and limp slowly towards me, and I said to him.

"What's wrong old lad? and I bent down to feel the leg he was favouring. Phil, I went cold all over when I examined it. It was a nasty gash — like a knife slash, the blood around the wound had congealed, but I could plainly see it went very deep. Well, I took one of the empty buckets and washed it in the stream, then dashed back to Smoky to see if he would let me wash the blood away, so I could see just how deep the wound was."

"I sent Irene over to the car to get some clean rags and some of that blue powder the vet gave us for cuts, lucky I still had some in the car."

"Then what did you do?" I asked.

Bert continued, "between us we managed to get the wound cleaned up, but it looked so nasty that I said to Irene, I think we'll go straight home and put a call through to the vet."

When they got back I told them to wash up while I called the vet. Our usual vet was on holiday, but his colleague came out straight away. Bert and Irene went back to the fields where he promised to meet them. He treated the wound and gave Smoky an injection and said he would treat him again the next day.

This treatment went on for several days, but to no avail, poor Smoky, he just got weaker and weaker until he couldn't stand.

The vet was kind! He did everything he possibly could. But a week later on the Friday morning he said to me ...

"I'm sorry! I've done everything possible, he's not going to pull through, it's blood poisoning! It looks like he's been stabbed! I think it best that you have him put down and out of his misery."

"Yes," I said, "I don't want him to suffer."

Smoky just lay there, looking up at me with such sad eyes.

I knelt down beside him, and although he must have been in great pain he managed to eat a little warm bran mash from the palm of my hand. I could hardly see him for tears and when I glanced up at the vet, he looked very sorrowful too.

"I suggest you go and sit in my car," he said. "I'll give you a lift home, phone your husband and ask him to make the necessary arrangements to have the gelding put down and taken away, I don't think you want to do it, do you?"

"No!" I said quietly. I found it hard to speak as a lump had formed in my throat.

I paid my last respects to Smoky and hurried out of the field to the vet's car, and before my family came home that evening I hid myself away.

Diane and Shirley came to see me the next day, they were very upset, but they insisted that I went with them to the new tack shop in Brentwood and between them they bought me a new green velvet riding cap. It was a very kind thought, but it didn't take the hurt away.

They say trouble always comes in threes, but I was ill prepared for the next bad news which came three weeks after Smoky's demise.

I was busy in the kitchen that fateful afternoon and not expecting visitors, so I was quite surprised when I heard a car pull up on the driveway. There was no knock upon my door to follow, so I went through the kitchen to the front room window, where I saw my son Anthony's car. I could see Pat and Anthony sitting there, but they seemed reluctant to get out, and I noticed that they never had the twins with them.

I opened the front door and called out to them.

"This is a nice surprise," I said. "Is it my birthday or something?"

"Where are the children? Is your mother looking after them?"

Neither of them answered, they jumped out of the car, pushed past me and ran into the house, their faces almost completely covered by large wet handkerchiefs.

I thought at first they were laughing.

I shut the door quickly and hurried after them into the house.

They were in the kitchen. Pat had collapsed across the table, her body racked with sobs, I looked with anguish at my son's face, it was grey, and his eyes were red and swollen.

"Good God!" I said. "Whatever's the matter?"

"Sit down Mum," he said, "we have some very bad news to tell you. One of the twins, little Debbie, died last night."

"How?" I screamed. The tears cascading down my cheeks.

"The doctor called it a cot death — whatever that means," he said between sobs.

I don't remember the rest of our action or conversation too clearly. This was happening to someone else I thought, not us. It was something I didn't want to believe. I do remember vaguely phoning the immediate family, then doing the usual British action in times of stress. I made some tea!

Then I disappeared to the stables where I sought solace as I cried my heart out on Frosty's shoulder, and there I stayed like a coward, until Irene and Bertie came home.

After the funeral, it seemed as though fate brought something about to keep me from brooding.

DUMPER TRUCKS ... BULLDOZERS ... AND MEN WITH PICKS AND SHOVELS...

They came early one morning and started to tear down the chainlink fence at the end of the road, the fence which separated my house from the paddock. Being nosey — well, who wouldn't be seeing that kind of activity, I leaned out of the bedroom window and shouted down to one of the labourers.

"Hi! What's going on?"

He looked up in alarm. "God, you startled me Missus," he said. "We're tearing down the fence."

"Yes! I can see that," I said. "What I want to know is — what for?"

"We're going to start building phrase three of this estate, it's going to be called Barley Field, and it will start about five feet from your house. That's why the fence has to come down — satisfied?"

"Thanks for the information," I said. "But Mr. Brian said when I bought this property that there would be no more houses built past mine — not in my lifetime. He evidently didn't think much of my chances of leading a long life — did he?"

There was no response to that remark. So, when Mr. Brian came by with the surveyor a few days later, curiosity got the better of me and I stopped to ask them about phrase three, and to thank Mr. Brian on his cheerful predictions about my short life-span.

In answer to my questions, he said.

"We are going to build some semi-detached houses on your side, and some four-in-a-row terraced houses facing them. The whole site will be formed in a semi-circle, leaving a gap in the centre. There, I am going to put five large detached houses. But their back gardens and double garages will be facing your road and their front entrances will be in Swan Lane."

"That's a funny bit of planning," I told him. "It certainly seems odd to me."

I left them to go about my own business. At the time I didn't think those back-to-front houses would mean anything to me.

However, when they were actually occupied, I was to become great friends with the family that moved into the centre house in Swan Lane.

Their name was Plum — Joan and Reg, they had two daughters, Angie and Veronica, two charming young ladies, there were also two sons, Michael and Timothy.

Joan and her daughter Angie were ardent horse lovers, which attracted me to them in the first place, and Joan's younger son Tim attended the same school as Ray. Later they were to go to the same boarding school together in the county town of Lincoln.

At first Joan never had a horse of her own, but she did drive a car — and so we compromised ....

She rode Bridgit — and I rode Frosty, and if I wanted to go shopping in town — we both rode in her car ...

However, it wasn't too long before she bought a horse of her own. A Welsh Cob, she called him Teddy. He was a light bay of fifteen-hands with a thick furry coat — just like a Teddy bear.

He was traffic proof, kind and gentle, but, oh so slow! His name should have been Plodder, for that was his usual pace. He was always lagging far behind. So while Joan progressed on Bridgit, Angie accompanied us on Teddy, and many a mile we traversed the Essex countryside together.

One day we even managed to get mixed up in a shoot on Lord Peters Country estate. My! what a day that turned out to be.

We were only interested in going out for a short hack, until Angie suggested we ride over to the Fiddlers (a pub near Winningale) for some lunch. "And maybe," she said, "we'll have time to go through the bridle path through Lord Peters land, it's very pretty scenery!

"Is it okay if we go through there?" I asked.

"Yes," she said, "we are allowed!"

And so we did.

After enjoying a drink and some lunch standing outside the Fiddlers, we left the horses tied up and grazing on the common land facing the pub.

"Righty Ho!" said Joan when she had finished her lunch, "I did enjoy that and it's only twelve-thirty so we shall have plenty of time between now and four o'clock to hack through old Peters bridle path; and the horses might enjoy a fast trot — we might even get a steady canter out of them."

The day was quite cool, but we had dressed warmly for the occasion. The air was crisp and dry after the previous night's rain.

It made a good day for riding, not only for us was the day ideal, but also for other sportsmen to participate.

The bridle path through the estate was quiet and peaceful, all we could hear was the twittering of the birds and the steady clip-clop of the horses hooves and our light-hearted banter. We did a rising trot, a sitting trot and a short canter for most of the way out, until I was surprised to see the sky darken over and I thought I felt a spot of rain. I turned to Joan and said. "It looks like rain, and it is getting late, I think we should turn back now — don't you?"

"Yes," Joan replied. "I think we've been out long enough and we do have a distance to go before we get home. I don't know about rain," she continued, "but, I thought I heard a clap of thunder in the distance."

"Funny now you come to mention it." I said "I thought I heard it too, only it didn't sound loud enough for thunder — more short and sharp — like a car backfiring." We stopped to listen for a minute or two then hearing nothing more we started to make our way back thinking no more about it.

"Let's have a quick canter now," I said to Joan and Angie, "Okay girls."

"Sure!" they said. "Lead on!"

We were five-hundred yards or so away from the end of the path when the sounds of dogs barking and people shouting became audible. Then harsher sounds followed, this time I definitely recognized the sounds as gunfire as it grew closer. I knew there was something going on, so I pulled Frosty up sharply and reined in looking over my shoulder to see how far back my friends were.

Bridgit was coming up fast, but Teddy who was half trotting half cantering — was well behind.

"I think it's a shoot, somewhere close by," I said to Joan who had reined in beside me. "It certainly sounds like it," I said.

Angie who had pushed Teddy on now drew in beside Bridgit. They were both puffing, Angie's cheeks were very red and she had a worried expression on her face as she turned to me and said.

"What's all the mad rush for? Poor old Ted's worn out!"

"Angie," I said, "there could be a shooting party in progress."

"Oh Golly!" she said as she looked about her as if expecting to see a mad gunman emerge from a nearby clump of trees.

We never had a chance for any further conversation, as from behind a small coppice several men with shotguns appeared, followed by two furiously yelping dogs, and behind them a party of men carrying heavy sticks.

They moved in towards us, the dogs barking and snapping around the horse's legs. Bridgit gave one black and white collie a swift kick with her back legs. Frosty fidgeted pulling on the bit but I held him firmly as we stood our ground. Poor Teddy was a mass of nerves. He puffed and snorted and jumped up and down, and reared up on his back legs, Angie had a job to hold him.

A tall thin man detached himself from the others. He looked very smart and well dressed in a sportsman-like fashion, but his face was almost purple. His mouth twitched, as did his bristly-red moustache. He advanced towards me menacingly, and with an immaculate yellow-gloved hand raised an accusing finger, pointed it in my direction.

"What the hell are you doing in here!? Don't you know this is all private property!?" he said. "There's a shoot on! Don't you know it's bloody dangerous?"

I glared at him!

"What question do you wish me to answer first?" I asked him.

"Don't be bloody impertinent." He shouted.

"Get off my property now, or you're liable to get shot!"

That did it, his last words made my blood boil.

"First of all," I said, looking at him with distain.

"Are you Lord Peter?"

"No," he yelled.

"Then who are you," I asked him. "And by whose authority do you turn us away from a public bridle path?"

"And secondly," I said, "my friends and I are out riding! there's no law against that — is there?"

"And," I went on, "if there's a shoot going on, why didn't you put up a notice about it, preferably at each end of the path.

"And," I finished with a flourish.

"I've got a shotgun, and I can use it, so if you're threatening these horses you will have to answer to me!

"And further more," I told him, "any more of your course language and I shall bring a constable back with me."

"Ha! Ha!" one of the beaters shouted. "Who are you going to get, a mountie!"

I ignored him but said loudly to Joan and Angie, so that all the men could hear.

"Come on girls, who wants to ride in their silly old grounds anyway! stupid lot of old codgers playing with guns and shooting down defenceless birds."

"Well," said Angie, with a giggle. "I expect it's the only kind of birds they're likely to get.

Joan and I laughed heartily at the joke as we told our mounts to trot on. However, a nasty-looking hunter who must have taken umbridge at Angie's joke, so much so, that he discharged his weapon just as we turned to ride away. The result was catastrophic for Angie.

Slow-coach Teddy, tore off down the path as fast as his fat little legs would carry him, and Joan followed at a gallop on Bridgit.

The men laughed! Frosty never moved. He was used to guns going off, as Bert often went rabbit shooting in the fields at Blackmore.

I knew the girls would be able to steady their mounts before they reached the end of the estate, so I rode slowly over to the man who had discharged the gun and said to him.

"That wasn't very clever was it? I hope you are proud of yourself, you haven't heard the last of this. I assure you. Next time I see Lord Peter, I shall tell him."

I never let on that I never knew Lord Peter from Adam.

"And I'll tell him what a course lot you are."

Some of the men looked sheepish and turned away.

The others stood there, almost defying me to stay for a further argument. I never gave them the pleasure.

Sitting up tall and straight in the saddle, I rode sedately away.

That was the first — and the very last time that I ventured into that scene of supposed quiet and tranquility.

The last ride into a shot-gun hunter's paradise .....

## Chapter Fifteen

# TWO TO GO A HUNTING

The early March winds do blow and the countryside is still held in the icy grip of winter. Cold frosty mornings, rainy afternoons, grey skies and colourless empty fields. All this seeking to depress the stoutest of hearts. When party times are over, and for the ardent worshippers of the sun, summer seems so far away. But for the farmers and the equestrian enthusiasts, there is always the joy of a good days hunting to look forward to, and the cub hunting starts off the season; for the novice, the first-time-to-hounds man and old Uncle Tom Cobbly and all.

The gathering takes place in the early morn and there's no special uniform worn, just a hard hat, hacking jacket and a strong pair of riding boots. The whole idea of the cub hunting is to train the young hounds. I seldom attended those affairs but some of my younger friends did. Diane and Shirley, and Jane and Tina and a few others from the local riding school. I liked to wait for the big show!

So I was hardly surprised one morning at hunting time, when Joan popped her head around my kitchen door — shouting!

"Tally Ho! Tally Ho!"

"Com on in Joan," I called to her. "What's all this Tally Ho business about?" As if I didn't guess.

"Ah!" she said. "I've come to see if you would like to do a spot of hunting next Wednesday? Do you think you can find the time? We shall have to make an early start!"

"It sounds very tempting, do come in and we can discuss it," I answered her somewhat craftily, thinking to entice her in to help me fill up the feed buckets.

"Sorry old bean, I can't stay now, I have to go into Brentwood to take some shoes in for repair. Can I get you anything whilst I'm in town?" she asked.

"Not really," I replied. "But if you're taking shoes in for repair you can take Frosty's while you're about it," I was feeling rather witty.

"Ha! Ha! Very funny," Joan replied, "I'll tell you what I will do though,

I'll deliver a message to the blacksmith for you, how does that suit?''

"Off you go!'' I said, "Before you get too clever, but pop in on your way back and I'll have a cup of tea ready, we can talk about the hunt then.''

"Will do!'' she chortled as she dashed away.

Joan always dashed everywhere, but it didn't rub off on her Cob Teddy, how she ever found the patience to persevere with him I could never figure out.

However, she did return some time later for her promised cup of tea and a brief talk about the hunt and all the arrangements that would have to be made before we went.

The day of the hunt saw me up with the dawn, for in truth, I hadn't slept a wink the night before. Why? Well I always managed to get butterflies in my stomach, no matter what venture I embarked upon.

But there, the thoughts of a days hunting in the wide open (usually forbidden) territory, somehow dispelled my fears.

Now in this venture of mine, Irene had decided to take a day's leave of absence from work, not to accompany me, but to get the mare ready and maybe follow up later with Angie to watch, and if she had time to spare she would help me with the household chores.

For this I was grateful. So while I went over the stables to put the halter on Bridgit and lead her over, Irene did the dishes, and during my absence Irene told me that Joan had telephoned.

"What did she want?'' I asked.

Irene replied, "She wanted to know if you would like to use her garage to clean Bridgit down, she said she thought it would save you from getting your boots dirty by walking across the muddy field, and besides, Angie would like to help.''

"That's fine.'' I said. "So if you would like to take Bridgit over there, I can be getting myself ready.''

A few moments later, Irene with Bridgit in tow departed, carrying her assortment of curry combs and brushes.

I was to follow later with the bridle and saddle.

Now as I explained before, the Plumb's twin garage was situated at the end of their garden, the entrance facing our road. It was a large concrete building with two separate car ports, with metal up-and-over doors, and the whole structure was divided evenly and separated by a concrete wall with an open access of roughly three and a half foot across and five feet in height and on that disastrous morning this opening proved to be our salvation.

My daughter had no trouble persuading the mare to stand just inside the first garage, but like all animals in strange places, after a while, she began to fidget, so Irene thought it would be better for all concerned if she closed the garage door.

This proved almost fatal: down came the heavy metal door with a mighty clang and up went Bridgit's back legs — one terrific kick dented and disfigured the door — beyond all recognition. And as an exit it was useless....

I was ready early, so I picked up the bridle and saddle, stepped out of the house and made tracks for Joan's garage.

I was almost there when I heard this terrible racket.

I could hear shouts! Yells! and loud clangs like a hammer on metal. Then shouts of — "Hold her still! Watch her legs! Keep her head down! — Oh crikey! Can't you open the ruddy door?! No! it's stuck!"

There seemed to be pandemonium going on behind the grey metal garage door ..... panic reigned .....

Somehow I guess what had happened, the door must have fallen down. I never guessed that someone had actually shut it — not with a horse inside. Seeing there was nothing I could do from that end I dropped the bridle and saddle on the ground and ran though the alley to Joan's side gate, into her garden and straight into the small side door of her garage.

Sizing up the situation and looking at the small opening and then at the size of Bridgit, I thought, this is going to be a hell of a ticklish job. I said to Joan. "How the devil are we going to get her out of there? There's no way out by the main door, it's stuck! Unless of course, you have an extremely large can opener."

"It's not funny," said Joan, almost in tears. "What on earth am I going to tell Reg?"

I didn't have an answer to that one, but I did suggest to her that a bucket of oats might do the trick.

"Are you serious?" Joan replied. "Oats! she's hotted up enough already, it's only the door that's damaged at present; God help me if she kicks the whole building down!"

Just then Joan had a brain-wave. She rushed into her kitchen, filled a large bowl with her finest vegetables, knowing that a display of food such as that — would be the quickest way to calm the poor creature down.

The idea worked fine! After much coaxing and cajoling, and when the mare had her head deeply entrenched within the bowl, Joan grabbed her head-collar; and with one shaking hand on the bowl and the other hand

*Phil on Bridget*

attached to Bridgit's collar she walked slowly backwards towards the opening, talking quietly to the animal all the time. The greedy mare was so engrossed with eating that Joan was able to ease her through the aperture without her even being aware of it ... and from there, through the other part of the garage to the street to where I waited with Irene. Not really knowing how! Who! or in what condition the victors would emerge.

I hated to think what Reg would say when he got home. I felt very sorry for Joan, I knew Reg wasn't very keen on horses, he tolerated them for his wife's sake.

Naturally we had to pay for the damage, but I think what Irene hated the most was the lecture she received from her father, especially when he found out the cost of the repairs.

I, however, was immune to calamity at this stage of my dealings with horses, and togged-out as I was in my best riding habit, there was no way that I was going to forego the day's hunting.

We would be late for the meet, that was for sure, so once I had left the hard-surfaced road and was making for Gypsy Lane, which in turn merged into the soft, narrow path of Dagwood Lane, I put Bridgit into a canter until we reached the stables where Joan boarded Teddy. And there was Joan and Angie, they had proceeded me there — in their four-wheeled vehicle — busily taking-up Teddy.

Mounted and away, Teddy was more of a slow-coach than ever and no amount of encouraging words or taps with the crop would induce him to quicken his pace, so, we had to take a short cut across the fields to catch up with the other hunters.

It was a shame, as we would miss the partaking of a wee dram from the stirrup cup, and the first sight of the meet: the gathering of the mounted riders, the hunt master, the whipper-in with his full regalia of hounds. And the gentlemen who we knew would look splendid in their pink, well-tailored hunting coats, white jodhpurs and high, tan boots.

The ladies and their children of course, would be dressed in smart, black riding habits, hard-topped velvet hats and light-fawn jodhpurs showing above long, black leather boots. White stocks would be neatly tied at the throat and yellow-gloved hands would be holding the reins, usually an ebony-handled crop would be clasped in the rider's hand to complete the ensemble.

Quite a picture to be sure!

The turn-out was quite large that day.

There were farmers and their wives, businessmen, members of the local riding club, retired gentle folk, and a few young children. In fact, anyone who could keep up with the hounds, pay their dues and conduct themselves in the traditional manner befitting a member or a guest of the "Essex Farmer's Union Hunt Meet".

Any awkward horses or ponies that were not adversed to dishing out a kick or two were politely asked to keep to the rear of the party; and such an aggressive steed should display a bow of red ribbon attached to his tail — for all to see.

Silence in the hunting field is a must. It is no place for idle chatter, and to ride ahead of the Master is an unforgivable sin, as is the exasperating terminology of calling the hounds — dogs. To be late for the meet is considered highly impertinent and extremely ill-mannered.

That was why — Joan and I — kept to the rear when we caught-up to the hunt.

We were late in arriving, and I for one, possessed an aggressive mount — no way could I tie a ribbon on Bridgit's tail. And of course — Bridgit hated dogs — hounds or otherwise! As for Teddy, well, we never imagined he would be anywhere else except at the back — but you can never tell with horses.

The hunt servants had gone before to open the gates and to keep an eye on stragglers or any trouble-makers with banners, depicting blooded-huntsmen and sad pictures of the persued fox.

The morning was cold with a nip of frost in the air, and we set out on a ground that was hard and ridged from the turned, ploughed furrows. Leafless trees shed cracked and brittle branches as we rode by. A few crows squawked. Other birds flew the hedgerows to seek shelter from the flying clods of earth from the horses hooves. The horses, excited by pastures new, galloped hard in the wake of nose-to-earth sniffing hounds while the riders hunched forward in the saddle across their mount's necks, steering them ever onward. The hot breath of horse and pony rose upwards, like puffs of fine smoke, soaring into the damp cold air. I watched for Joan and Teddy as the pace quickened. Yes! There she was, standing up in her irons, her eyes protruding from her chalk-white face as beans on stalks.

For Teddy, usually a diddly-dawdler, shot past me going hell-for-leather in his efforts to outrun the other horses.

Bridgit spotted his rear end go flashing by, and not wanting to lose sight of her companion, she galloped after him like a bat out of hell. A thick coppice wood loomed ahead of us and to avoid slamming into a tree she veered quickly, and with two legs on the high ground and the other two in the furrow, making my seat lop-sided and dangerous we high-tailed it around the perimeter of the next two fields. Then through the open gate at a gallop at the same time as three other horses; and, as I was on the side of the gate-post and being astride a wide mount, my knee caught the full impact as it crashed into the post.

Bridgit didn't seem to care. She no doubt was just beginning to enjoy herself — but I felt sick.

Next came a mad skirmish through the woods, where there were many fallen trees to leap over.

Now a horse doesn't stop to ask you. "Do you think you can jump over this one?" So, if you try to avoid it by ducking under a low, hanging branch and catching the peak of your cap on it, you could stand a good chance of being almost strangled by the elastic chinstrap.

That! I suppose the excited animal thinks — is your misfortune.

It is sometimes difficult to keep tabs on your friends in the field, the best time to look around for them is in the waiting periods, when the hounds go to ground to stop to pick up the scent.

I didn't actually see Joan again until some time later, because it was Tally Ho! and away we all went again.

But when I did eventually discover her, she looked positively worn out.

I quietly made my way over to her and in a sound akin to a whisper she said:

"I say Phil, let's call it a day, shall we? I'm jolly well tired out and so is poor old Ted."

Teddy looked fine to me, he was still pulling on the bit and I could see he was eager to be off on the charge again, but I knew how Joan felt, and my knee was still pretty sore.

"Did you have any trouble with Bridgit?" she asked. "Kicking I mean."

"Well she had a try," I told her. "That young boy of Mr. Longs, I did warn him not to stay too close to me, but he said he was frightened and he wanted me to look after him, I told him to find a hunt servant and he would take care of him."

"Well his mother's with him," Joan said.

"Didn't you hear his mother fell at the first fence?"

"No," Joan replied. "I was too busy trying to control Teddy."

"I know what you mean." I said. "He surprised me! tearing off like that, what did you give him this morning? Two buckets of oats."

When the hue and cry went up again, Joan and I slipped cautiously away, we trotted back the way we had come, by way of The Thatcher's Arms.

"I think we've earned a drink Phil, don't you?"

I nodded in agreement. It had been a long and eventful day.

# Chapter Sixteen

# FAREWELL TO A FRIEND

In the September of nineteen-seventy-five, my dear companion and friend Bridgit seemed to be suffering from an acute pain in her right hip, she began to hobble around favouring her right side. I called the vet, and after examining her he gave me some cortisone tablets for her.

"They will relieve the pain for some time," he said. "But I shouldn't ride her on a hard surface or trot her on the road.

"I know you can't walk her on the crown of the road, it's too dangerous! And, it would cause her great discomfort if you walk her by the kerbside, as the slope towards the pavement would be awkward for her gait. She has an arthritic hip, you know, and if it gets worse, which it probably will do — you won't be able to ride her at all — and eventually you will have to have her put down." I told him "I just couldn't part with her, not yet."

"I didn't ask you to," he said. "Just ride her gently in the fields and I'll look in on her from time to time, but she won't winter-out this year."

"She's been a good mare!" I said "Healthy and strong! It was a great pity we lost her foal; we did try again you know, from a stallion over at Navestockside."

"Did you?" he said.

"Yes," I replied. "But after two attempts I brought her back again: she didn't want to know. Do you know, they kept her in a stable with a cobble-stoned floor for two weeks. Do you think that standing on a floor of that kind for so long started off her arthritis?"

"Hard to say." he said. "But it wouldn't help any."

"I shall miss riding her out," I told him. "Even though she gave me many a fright — and the predicaments she got herself into you wouldn't believe." He laughed! "Yes! I can quite believe it." he said.

"Look! I have a little time to spare this morning, why don't you make me a nice cup of tea, then you can tell me all about it."

We went back to the house. I made tea and while he sipped his tea at the kitchen table I related to him one of her many exploits.

Like the time we were out together hacking on a quiet peaceful summer's afternoon.

"I was so thirsty! all the Inns were closed, and the only place we came upon that was open for business was the little cottage-come-sweet shop over by Highwoods. Do you know it?" I asked him. "Can't say that I do," he said. "But carry on."

Well, I continued with my story. "I left Bridgit tied up outside the shop by looping her reins loosely over an old wooden post by the open door.

"I swear I hadn't left her for more than a minute. I was looking over the ice-lollipops in the deep freeze, when suddenly, the old lady serving behind the counter, gave out a piercing scream!

"I looked at her in surprise. Surely, I thought, my face wasn't all that frightening. — No! she was looking past me and over my shoulder. Her face had turned as white as a sheet, and her eyes like tea-saucers, were large, wide and staring. She looked so terrified, I was afraid to turn round. But I did ... and there ... as large as life ... was Bridgit! Before I could do, or say anything, she pushed me to one side, dived her head straight in to the open freezer and started to rummage through the ice creams. She found the one she fancied, and proceeded to crunch on it as fast as she could, and before she had finished one, she was busily sorting out another. A large chocolate-peppermint-cream this time.

"I watched in fascination for a minute or two while she gobbled up a few more. Rooted to the spot, I stood there watching, until the sound of a hysterical voice brought me back to earth.

"Get her out of here! Get her out of here! for Gaw'd Sakes! the old woman yelled. Easier said than done, I thought. But how?

"I picked up the trailing reins that were broken in the middle (she must have broken them when she forced them off the post) I tied them together, while she still had her head in the ice-creams. I yanked her head up and forced her backwards towards the shop door.

"But alas! Halfway through ... she got stuck. I couldn't push her in or out — the saddle was wedged fast."

"Don't panic! Don't panic!" I said to the near-hysterical shop owner. "I'll get her out of there — Don't fret! You hold her reins and if you'll allow me I'll go through your house and around to the front entrance and I'll try to take her saddle off.

"Maybe I'll get her out then.

"Have you got a back door?"

"Ye-Ye-Yes!" she stammered. "Go through the shop and into the kitchen, the back door's on the right-hand side."

"Thanks," I said, as I dashed through the shop and out of the back door, but in my haste I tripped over her Ginger Tom Cat.

He awoke with a start and tore off before me letting out a series of banshee wails. I stumbled, and to stop my fall I grabbed hold of a small ornamental table which fell with an almighty crash taking the potted-palm-plant that adorned it down with it, spilling the contents of dried leaves and earth all over the carpet. I tried to set the table and plant to rights, and when I eventually got to where the mare was, she hadn't moved an inch.

I wondered if the store-keeper was still feeding her face with goodies. Easing the saddle gently I finally managed to slip it off to lay it down on the grass verge out of harm's way.

I didn't want her treading on it, if — and when — she emerged.

I doubled back to the mare and pushing and shoving with all my might I heave-hoed her backwards through the door and out into the sunshine, blowing out my cheeks with a sigh of relief.

I was just about to deliver her a lecture on her greediness, when I noticed the state of her nose. It was covered with a sweet sticky substance, and believe it or not, the stick from the lollipop was still sticking out of her mouth. She seemed loath to part with it.

Outside on the green a crowd of young children had gathered, presumably on their way home from school.

"What's she doing in there?" One cheeky lad remarked.

"Did she pay for those lollies Missus?" he asked me as he jumped up and down with glee.

I never answered him, I felt foolish. I hastily put on Bridgit's saddle, mounted up and rode swiftly away.

I sent a letter to that shop — by pony express. Shirley delivered it, I didn't dare.

The vet smiled! "You should write a book on your adventures," he said. "But I'm sorry, I'll have to go now. It's a shame the mare's sick but I know you'll learn to cope with it. Next time I see you I hope it will be in happier circumstances.

"But tell me," he said, "just for curiosity's sake, did you ever go back to that shop?"

"What do you think," I told him, as my parting shot.

It was to be later that evening that Bert, Irene and myself had a long discussion about Bridgit's arthritis — and what we intended to do about it. "We'll keep her for awhile and see what happens," Bertie said, "and in the meantime I'll speak to Vic and ask him if we can use his spare stable for the winter, the one in the top field nearest the water-trough. I'll offer him some extra hay!

Vic agreed. "Sure you can use it," he said. "We don't want the poor old dear suffering out in the cold all winter. Do we Bertie?"

She'll be company for young David's horse, the big grey that's up there now! Young David he spoke of, was his neighbour's son, who was training to become a blacksmith; he was to do some shoeing for us later on. His sister Nicholia, was just a young school girl then, she was later to become one of my daughters-in-law.

So the problem of Bridgit's wintering out was solved; and during that summer and late fall she grazed contentedly in the fields at Doddinghurst, and some evenings Shirley was to be seen riding her gently around the fields with Cobber, jealously watching, and sometimes he would walk to the fore, with ears menacingly well back — to give Bridgit the kick-back treatment.

But with all the care and medicines, her condition didn't improve.

She was a model patient, taking her pills without fuss, she even asked for them when offered, by stamping her fore-hoof three times, a trick I once taught her which she never forgot. I knew I could never ride her or take her out hunting again — and one day there would be an empty stall.

So when riding out on Frosty by the stables at Highwood, I would let my eyes stray over to their grazing fields, hoping to spot a likely new mount to replace my old chum.

Meantime, the summer came and the horse-shows were in full swing. There were showing events for Lady Jane, and show-jumping and gymkhana events for Frosty. And another young friend came to join our band of riders.

Her name was Sylvia. She was a good all-rounder at showing in the show-jumping classes, and in the ring at gymkhana.

Now Shirley's dad had just bought her a Chestnut mare of fifteen-hands, a pretty little thing, road trained and a willing jumper.

So while Shirley progressed on her new mount, Sylvia offered to compete for us on Frosty, and the proudest moment for us and for the girls parents, was when Sylvia, on Frosty, won first place for the very first time in the showing class. Bertie proudly recorded this event on his new home movie machine.

Sylvia and her younger sister accompanied me on many of my riding excursions during the next few years.

My new riding companions had mounts of their own, the younger girl rode a black and white fourteen-hand pony, and her sister rode a fourteen-two-hand gelding with a coat of burnished gold, just like a bright new penny. He was as active as Frosty and when we took to the gallops at High Ongar, it was always a neck to neck finish to the race. So it was no wonder that Frosty and Mr. Rusty won so many rosettes and trophies, a faster pair of ponies would have been hard to find; as we rode those ponies so often, it was small wonder that the blacksmith was a regular visitor to both our stables. Which brings to mind the blacksmiths we engaged for over a period of twenty years.

Our first introduction to a tradesman of this fine and noble calling; well, noble I say loosely, because brave or courageous would be more appropriate words.

Mr. Kelly our first blacksmith, was certainly brave, I'll say that for him, especially after his first whiskey, which lingered on his breath as a tell-tale sign.

He was also master of the fine art of show-jumping, and he had many pictures which he proudly displayed upon his caravan-home wall. Depicting him and his various mounts in action.

Born and raised in Ireland, he had that certain Irish look about him; he was blonde and blue-eyed, and he spoke with an un-mistakable Irish lilt; with a touch of the blarney to match. I enjoyed listening to his many tales of Ireland, horses, and his travels, the latter he related to me either while shoeing a horse or joining me in an after-work-cuppa! He was a likeable character, easy to get along with, and always a gentleman, in front of me anyway.

His half-hearted cusses were never too crude; in fact, some were quite humorous.

He would come very early in the morning in his old land-rover-come jeep, drop down its tail-board with a clatter, and with a giant heave lift off the anvil and then the small brazier; still warm from the last firing. The bellows followed, and within minutes the fire glowed a fiery red.

"Get me a bucket of cold water, please Missus, there's a good lass," were his first words to me after a cheerful greeting.

"I have it here already," I would tell him.

"Then go and get whoever's first 'Me gal!" he would say.

I waited for his next request before I moved to do his bidding, it was always the same. "I'll have the easiest one first! I'll have the old lad, Frosty I think; Hoity! Toity! fidgety, jibbet, Lady Muck Jane ..... I'll leave until last."

The day I broke the sad news to him about Bridgit, he was genuinely upset.

"You're doing the right thing by her, Missus! I know it's hard, but it's the kindest thing."

We talked about her for a bit and got to reminiscing. He said he always remembered the day that he promised to teach me to jump her in the field beside the house, before the new houses were built.

"Do you remember that Sunday afternoon?" he said.

"I'll say I do," I replied.

He came across to the house from the Shepherd Inn, it was about two o'clock — just after closing time, so I guessed he'd had a few pints of beer.

"Are you ready M'e gal?" he asked. "Then get the old mare out, tack her up, and I'll join you in a jiffy —"

When next I saw him, he was advancing towards me brandishing a long riding whip.

"Watch out!" I told him. "You'll scare the life out of Bridgit with that thing." "Never mind about her," he said.

"You start riding around me in a wide circle; get her into a trot!"

I meekly complied. "Now," he said. "Loop up the reins, and tie them into a knot in front of you, take your feet out of the stirrups and put your hands on your head.

"No! don't stop going round," he shouted. I looked at him rather peculiar, wondering what this kind of activity was going to accomplish. I was soon to find out ...

He motioned me to trot-on and cautioned me to keep my hands on my head where he could plainly see them; and on no account was I to take them down. This seemed easy, as I gripped the saddle with my knees and stared straight in front of me, so as not to lose my balance.

Things were going well, and I was still trotting blissfully around, when suddenly, out of the blue, I thought I heard the loud hiss of a snake. Bridgit jumped into air, four hoofs, literally leaving the ground as Mr. Kelly's long whip went into action catching the startled mare across the rump.

Boy! was she mad. She left the imaginary show ring behind, then cantered off to the far corner of the field where she turned, made towards her tormentor, whinnied loudly, and snorted like a bull. It surprised me that she never charged him!

Now whatever polish I had cleaned that saddle with, must have been akin to glue, because I never left it, but I did put my hands down mighty quick to grab a handful of mane and the tied-up bridle reins. "Let go! Let go! of those pesky reins," Mr. Kelly shouted as he ran towards me waving his whip. "Let go of those reins or I'll use this whip on you!"

I didn't know whether I was mesmerised — or just plain stupid. But I did as I was told. He told me to rein in and came over to me saying. "I've got to hand it to you Missus! I thought you'd come off of the old gal — long since — you've got a good seat! I'll teach you to jump her — next week.

"Will you! be dammed" I heard Bertie say, as he came striding across the field towards us. "No way!" he yelled.

He told me to get along to the house there was to be no more nonsense that day. "Or any other day" I heard him say to Mr. Kelly.

"You're fired!"

"That was a close shave for you that time," I told him.

"Yes," he said. "But a month after, he forgave me — didn't he?" and all was forgotten, and we had a good laugh about it!

However, a few weeks later and unknown to Bertie, Mr. Kelly called one afternoon, once again offering his services as a show-jumping instructor. I was interested, but Bridgit as usual wasn't too helpful. She did try to accommodate me by jumping over a few cavaletti's, but when it came to the three foot pole, she chickened-out. She cantered up to it willingly enough, then stopped dead in front of it. Then, after a hefty whack with my riding crop she took the jump at a stand; jumping awkwardly and landing heavily, throwing her head well back; which in turn, came in contact with my nose in the forward position.

Wham! stars appeared from out of a sunny sky. I slipped from the saddle dazed! my nose, bleeding profusely, and later that day I was to have a shiny, black eye. I had to tell Bertie what had happened and confess to being a party to Mr. Kelly's jumping lesson.

"That's right! don't listen to me when I tell you not to bother. You'll never make a show-jumper! and, you could have broken your neck. Old Mr. Kelly's had it this time. He's definitely got to go!"

"But you got around him again with your blarney, didn't you Mr. K?" Mr. Kelly smiled! "Sure I did M'dear but I'll not be with you much longer — I'm moving on!"

When I told Shirley he was going — she said. "Not to worry! I have just heard about two brothers who have started up a farrier business. Isabelle told me about them, they're going to shoe all her horses. Their names are Brian and Richard, I don't know their last name but I do have their telephone number.

"Thanks Shirley," I said. "I'll tell Bert, I'll ask him if he'll give the lads a try-out." And so, Brian and Richard took over!

They were punctual, quick and efficient, and they only drank tea or coffee. I was quite surprised when I first met the lads, they were tall, but slightly built, not at all like any pictures depicting blacksmiths that I'd ever seen. Dark of hair, bushy browed and with thick, hairy arms like Atlas or Hercules. But they were good at their job and that was the main thing.

They were nice lads, quiet and gentle, they never lost their temper with the horses, or hit them with a rasp like some I'd seen.

Brian and Richard did our horses for a good many years, but when the brothers parted company, Brian was so busy that we had to book him six weeks in advance. So, for some of the farriering we had David in to help us out.

I was usually the one to help when the farrier called.

I would fetch the water, make the tea and hold the horses, sometimes screwing up my nose in mock protest at the repugnant smell when hot metal hissed on hoof. Or, when one of the horses stood on my foot.

Most of the blacksmiths that I met were a grand bunch, but I never met a lady member of their calling. No doubt the day would come when I won't be needing them anymore. Whatever their sex.

But that time would be a few years hence.

Towards the end of the year in late September, my daughter Irene and Maggie's brother Brian were married. At long last, I was to have a son-in-law. I liked him from the start, we got on well together and we became great friends.

They couldn't very well live with us, as we had quite a few people already in residence, even Frosty dropped in one day for a few carrots. Irene and Brian had to move away. Not too far! But far enough for Irene to be unable to ride, or help out with the horses anymore, but Bert and I still had our memories. Before Irene left she sold her mare Foxy Lady to her dad. Foxy was quite a big lass by then so Bertie was able to ride out with me more frequently. And it was about this time too that I started to have health problems of my own. The doctor told me I had the same complaint as Bridgit. Arthritis in both hips.

I was scared to tell my husband in case he forbade me to ride. Then another thought crossed my mind.

I wondered if Bertie would have me put down?

I did have to go to the hospital for a few weeks. They never did anything about the pains in the hips but fixed me up with a surgical stiff collar. I never found out why, all I remember was some unkind person saying.

"Why! she looks like Horace Horse Collar in the Mickey Mouse Movies."

# Chapter Seventeen

# WELCOME MELODY

I always looked forward to the Autumn months in the country, especially when harvest time came around. I loved to see nature change the woodland leaves from deepest green to russet, gold and browns: and to see the white dog-daisies flowering beside the hedgerows and the luscious ripe fruit of the blackberry and elderberry. I often picked them to make apple and blackberry pie. I gave the elderberries to Hilda to make elderberry wine.

In the early afternoon the pale Autumn sunshine would make miniature rainbows in the rain-filled potholes by the wayside, and startled birds would fly out from the bushes as I rode by.

I watched with interest as the farmhands stacked straw bales to form a haystack, and call out to farmer Bell's sheepdog, stretched out by the farmyard gate. Riding over to Hilda's I would notice the last few unripened tomatoes sunning themselves on her windowsill along with whole bunches of onions strung up in a row.

To see in passing the Metson girls, Anne and Mary, sorting the potatoes from the stones on the conveyer belt in an open-topped truck in the farmyard.

"All right for some," they would shout. "What about getting down off that horse and giving us a hand?"

I often stopped to watch Don and Eddie working the big heavy balers in their open-necked, short-sleeved shirts, showing throat and arms as brown as berries from being exposed to wind and sun.

Sometimes they would call out to me. "We'er having a break soon would you like to join us for a sandwich or a mug of tea?"

If I did find the time to stop we would have a discussion about the weather and I would pray with them for the rain to hold off until the harvest was gathered in.

When the lads had finished all their own baling they would come over to the Doddinghurst fields and cut, turn and bale ours.

Gathering in the bales was a time for all the family to join in.

The bales at the far end of the field were loaded onto an old open truck. Bert would drive and the rest of us would stack. When the truck reached the top of the field the bales would have to be carted by hand to a special part of the stable, there, it would be covered by a large sheet of tarpaulin. The carting of the bales which were tied by binder twine made for many a sore palm, that's if you weren't wise enough to wear a heavy duty pair of gloves.

We always had a good crop of hay stored for the winter feeding as we alternated the grazing fields each year, but if we did experience a long hard winter, and the fodder ran low, we could always buy some more from the Metson's.

For the purpose of shifting hay and straw, Bert had purchased a reconditioned landrover (a vehicle resembling a war-time jeep) which, when loaded to the gunnals, appeared as a moving haystack. People would stop to stand and stare, as they did many a time when the landrover was ornamented with rosettes and ribbons, when we returned from a successful show.

There were a great many farms in our part of Essex, from dairy and chicken to crop farms, the latter growing wheat, oats, barley and rape. The rape field when ripe appeared to me as a vast yellow waving sea. Most crops were hedge-fenced and hedges divided the fields. The entrance was by a five-bar gate and for a trespasser it was a No! No! to climb over them, but some farmers allowed responsible riders to open the gates and ride through the land after the crops had been gathered in.

Such a place was the Co-operative farm, which covered an area of roughly three-hundred acres with four gates in between, so it was a real up and downer for Shirley, to get off her mount — to open and close each one. I wasn't that lazy, but, there was no mounting block handy and besides, Shirley was much young than I.

This stretch of farmland was a favourite place for us to ride through, as there were so many interesting things for us to see.

Cows grazing, (they were all ear-tagged and numbered) would push and jostle each other to get closer to the fence to see the horses.

Shirley would call out to them, "Hello! number forty-two" then we would giggle.

"You'd look funny," I would say to her. "If she asked you what number you were?"

We would continue on our way making towards the last gate just behind a quaint old pub called "The Wheatsheaf". There we would dismount, one of us would go in and buy the drinks, and also buy a small drink, pour it into a tray and give it to the horses, and if Shirley had enough cash with her, she would buy Cobber a bag of potato-chips, which he ate with relish, including the paper bag.

Rest and repast over, we mounted up and turned the horses to cross the main road to the long stretch of wide grass verge, then gallop all the way down to the Blackmore school, facing the house of my dear friend Margaret Mells.

One Sunday morning we happened to spot her outside her house tending her garden so we crossed over and stood by her gate to have a chat. On the grass verge by her gate she had placed a bushel basket of apples with a notice fixed to the top by a large wooden spoon. It read:—

"WIND-FALL APPLES HELP YOURSELF"

and that's just what Cobber and Bridgit did.

"You've got a pair of intelligent horses — girls," Margaret remarked. "Yes!" Shirley replied. "Didn't you known they could read?"

"Be off with you — clever clogs!" she answered. "Or you'll be late for your lunch."

"We've had it," we shouted gaily as we mounted up and rode off.

Other days we would arrange to meet Bert, accompanied by Allen (Shirley's boy friend). They would come to meet us by car to join us for a drink in "The Black Horse". I liked this pub on account of its large car-park leaving us plenty of space to stand with the horses. This time they happened to be Foxy Lady and Bridgit.

Now some of the patrons of the pub especially the young children who had to wait outside would come over to us and ask if they could stroke the horses.

Sometimes Shirley would lift up one of the youngsters and put them into the saddle on Cobber's back. That worked out fine, but one Sunday morning a real nosey parker came over — a right know-it-all, he engaged us for a while in conversation, then, he started to examine Bridgit from top to toe. He pointed out her finer points, that is until he came to her tail.

"Oh dear!" he said. "This tail could do with a good grooming!"

Nobody said a word! Shirley gave me a knowing wink. We both knew only too well how Bridgit felt about getting her tail brushed.

The nosey gent went on to say that he lived just behind the pub.

"That's my place over there! Where the donkeys are grazing."

I wasn't very interested in donkeys so I looked away to finish my drink. But that persistent person wasn't easily snubbed.

"I'll nip over and get a brush!" he informed me.

"You do that," I replied, losing all interest and hoping he'd take the hint and go away. "But don't say I didn't warn you, she doesn't like anyone touching her tail."

"Nonsense!" he said. 'I'll show you how it's done!"

He hastened away and I thought no more about him. However, he returned some five minutes later carrying a heavy wooden box, filled to the brim with a variety of curry combs and brushes.

"You're back then," I said. "Oh yes! did you think I'd forgotten lass? Just stand well back," he said importantly. "And leave her to me."

Well. I shall never forget the next thing that happened.

One minute he was crouched down low near the mare's back legs, his arms extended and with both hands poised with brush and comb.

I looked across at the others, and I saw Shirley staring back at me with her mouth pursed into a decisive OWW! her eyes raised towards the heavens. My eyes left my friend and returned to the busybody. I saw him take hold of Bridgit's tail with one hand and start a downward stroke with the brush with the other. The brush never travelled the whole way down ... I saw two ears lay well back and the two hefty black legs do a backward kick.

With a resounding yell! The tail-groomer did a backward-flip somersault straight into a pile of fresh manure that Cobber had left as his calling card for the garden conscious publican.

I tried hard not to laugh, but it was rather difficult. I felt sorry for the freshly-manured gentleman, but I did warn him.

He didn't appear to be too badly hurt, probably, just his dignity. I expect he would feel the pain later.

Bert and Allen picked him up and brushed him down with one of his own brushes. He didn't kick back — but hobbled away mortified.

Such were the Autumn adventures .....

Winter came in with a roar, with chill-to-the-bone North Winds and icy roads, and far-away-field-excursions ceased.

On fine days the horses were put out to graze covered in their New Zealand rugs and the only time they were trace-clipped was for important indoor-arena shows.

Christmas was a time for parties, in friends houses, or in the New Kelvedon Hatch Village Hall.

The Shepherd Inn, modernized by the new owner's mother and her married son, were full of new ideas. The Inn, now resembled a manor house, with red velvet curtains, thick red carpets in each bar and gleaming brasses now decorated the once bare walls: but the secret hiding place of Jack Shepherd the highwayman was never boarded up, and today it is still a tourist attraction. The bars were always full at the festive season and the villagers would gather together there for a chat and a singsong.

The Swan Inn — hadn't altered very much, except for the tenants.

The Inn had changed hands a number of times.

The brewery had sold a good part of the land around it so the stables had gone too.

Vic and Bert still shared the stables and the plot of land for grazing at the bottom of our gardens.

Poor Bridgit meanwhile, was finding it harder and harder each day to walk about, and in the following March we decided to have her put down. It was all very sad, and even now, I hate to dwell on that unhappy event; and when it did happen I never had the courage to be present or to bid her a last farewell; but I thought of her many times when I rode past our old hunting grounds.

However, life goes on, and one morning in April whilst riding past the Woodbine Stables at Highwood I happened to see a fine white Mare....

And so it came about, that another faithful steed joined our stables ....
Her name was MELODY ....

After a while we reverted to the shorter version of Melly and some unkind person — mentioning no names — used to call her Smelly Melly.

She stood fifteen hands high and pure white, with no markings.

She had the head of an Arab Steed — The tummy of a mare that had often foaled and a white silky tail and mane.

She was easy to catch — in fact, she would almost put her head into the bridle. There was no worry traffic-wise — well, only with milk-floats — and that was only when the milkman rattled the bottles into the crates. That was the only time she tried to throw me, when one of those noisy milk-floats followed close behind us all the way through Hay Green Lane. I knew then, that she could jump real high — and buck if she wanted to, but I wasn't interested in show-jumping her anyway.

Now Melly wasn't the only addition to our flock that year.

My son Anthony and his wife Pat were blessed with a son, such wonderful news for us all, after their last tragic loss!

They named him Anthony James, he was a dear little boy, with large blue eyes and a mop of blonde hair. Later, when the grandchildren were able to sit astride a mount, fond grandad, could be found most Sunday evenings running alongside Melly or Foxy Lady with a little grandchild perched on their backs.

# Chapter Eighteen

# ANNIVERSARY ADVENTURES

There is always some historic celebration taking place in England in one place or another: The Lord Mayor's Show, The Opening of Parliament, The Queen's birthday, and Royal Weddings. June 7th, 1977, the day commemorating Queen Elizabeth the Second's twenty-five years of reign, was certainly a day to remember.

Throughout the land from John O'Groats to Land's End, in cities, towns and hamlets, Her Majesty's loyal subjects had been busily preparing for the coming festivities for many months prior to the great event.

For shame! The great day dawned wet, cold and blustery.

High winds caught at the flags and buntings of red, white and blue sending them into a dancing frenzy. The fluttering of the pennants and the sound of the wind passing through the telegraph wires created eerie groans, like lost souls crying out in torment.

The combined elements that day became a force to be reckoned with.

"Oh joyful sunny June," did someone say?

And who was the clown who suggested a combined family ride and paper chase? (This popular event usually takes place on foot.) Where the hares, (fast runners) go forth with numerous pieces of paper with attached clues, and the hounds (as the following runners are called), collect the clues, and later meet at an arranged spot to compare notes and the winners are the ones who collect the most clues, they also collect prizes.

So you see, it seemed a stupid idea for such a day.

However, a few phone calls and two hours later, a motley crowd of shivering riders and excited mounts assembled on the green outside the Swan Public House, including myself, Bert, Irene and friends, Shirley, Dianne, Joan and Angie, and several others, about twenty riders in all. Word had spread that there might be fun and prizes. One never knew what to expect on those excursions.

As it was so cold, the publican suggested that we all partake of an unofficial stirrup-cup, the beverage usually reserved for hunt-meets. I admit I did indulge in rather a large measure of the fiery liquid to keep warm and to steady my nerves, thinking, that the journey could prove to be lengthy and maybe even hazardous. The planned route for the ride covered roughly eight miles up and along the Blackmore Road to Jericho House, (the favourite one time hunting lodge of Henry VIII,) on the outskirts of Blackmore Village. All went well until our band of riders came to the football field, where groups of young children with their doting fathers were gathered on the green, flying kites.

These large and colourful objects were fine entertainment for the excited village children, but not for the horses.

No way! The ever increasing gusts of wind blew the kites towards the road ahead, high over the heads of the oncoming riders.

Some horses shied, others whinnied or turned tail and fled back the way they had come. My mount Melody forsook all others, she reared and bucked a bit. Then a galloping we did go.

It took all of my strength and much coaxing to stop her and calm her down. By the time the others had collected their mounts, I was at the next focal point; the old Barn, on the Chelmsford Road next to the White Horse Inn, another drinking place, but this time it really was for medicinal purposes. I wasn't the only one either that needed sustaining, the gentlemen followers and instigators of the proposed on-horseback paper chase were already installed within the warmth of the pub's parlour. On hearing our approach they left their congenial surroundings, emerging with trays of lager and crisps for the brave explorers who were still ruffled from the kite-flying experience. We wondered what other fates awaited us after we proceeded on?

There were no more stops for refreshments until we gained access to the large tract of forest land by the open heath at High Woods opposite The Merry Fiddlers Inn.

However, to move on to the paper chase. We had already chosen partners, not just to accommodate the riders but to try to equalize the size of the mounts. I chose Joan, although Teddy was slow he was extremely good at opening gates, well at least he would stand steady so Joan never had to dismount.

"Back a bit! Forward a bit! Steady boy! Steady!" she would say; and old Teddy would wait patiently while Joan looped the string over the gate.

When we finally reached the starting point of the chase the noon sky had taken on a brighter hue, and as we gathered beneath the dripping wet branches of the Larchwood and the Beechwood trees the sun shone for a while, bathing the riders faces in a criss-cross pattern as the wind played havoc amidst the leafy branches. A tall young woman on a chestnut filly rode over to take command.

"Hello everyone," she said. "Can you all hear me? The hares I've been told, have been away for an hour or so, that's long enough, so, what do you say? Is it time we went after them?"

"Which way were they headed Miss Tomms?" someone asked.

"They were going to Highwoods," she said.

"They will probably cross the road and continue through the bridle-path behind the Viper's Arms. And, I don't wish to see anyone going in there for clues!" There was a general titter at her last remark. "However," she went on, "I understand, due to the windy weather, the clues will be affixed to the trees and not left on the ground, so keep a sharp lookout. Bring them back to me when you think you have collected enough. The first couple back with the most number of clues will claim the prize! Have you all got that? Do I make myself clear?"

"Perfectly," said a young girl on a copper-coloured pony. "That's if we don't get blown off our horses first!"

It was Sylvia, with her partner Shirley, but Shirley when she spoke, seemed to be more interested in the prize.

"I hope it's something to eat," she said. "I'm starving! and so is Cobber."

"That's nothing new," I said, butting in on her complaints.

"Miss Tomms seemed anxious for us to start. "Off you go everyone," she said. "Have a good time!"

In spite of the weather, the chase was fun, I always enjoyed riding through the woods and the traffic-free bridal path.

I did notice that some of the others that passed us were trotting out briskly, but Joan and I intended to take our time.

We saw Irene and Bert go by and they waved to us as they took a different path through the woods. Bert had always kidded me that he was from Red Indian stock, so, maybe he had seen tracks going in that direction. But I, being short sighted, relied on my partner to search the tree trunks for clues; and, she was successful, for within the hour we had collected quite a number. Some wet, some sticky and some with words that were almost obliterated, where we dropped them in the mud. Poor Joan, she was up and down so many times on Teddy's back — like a Yo! Yo!

Teddy wasn't at all pleased! Well who would be — having a muddy booted-toe digging in his ribs every five minutes, as Joan dismounted to retrieve her fallen clues.

After a time, my jacket was soaked and my trousered knees very damp, so I decided I'd had enough of collecting bits of damp cards, prizes or no. So I said to Joan, "I think we should turn back now! I feel shivers coming on and I don't want to catch cold."

"Fine! suits me!" Joan replied. "But I say Phil! Have you got another bag to put my clues in? My bag is falling to pieces."

"Yep! I've got just the thing," I told her, as I pulled out a brown paper carrier bag from my jacket pocket.

My partner leaned towards Melody, and as I opened the bag she dropped her clues inside.

"Come on Phil! I'll race you back!" she cried, as she spurred Teddy into action. I had never seen him go so fast — not since the day of the hunt. Melody tore after him ... and that was how we managed to be the first two back upon the scene; and as we galloped up to the organizers laughing, and breathless, we shouted in harmony "I think we must be the first back," as we waved the soggy wet bag, in front of their eyes.

"So you are," said Mr. Price, who was the father of one of the riding school girls.

"My! you're wet," he said. "Have you seen the mud on your boots Joan? How did you manage to get in that state?"

"She dropped some of her clues in a mud hole," I told him. "And rather than lose them she jumped down from her horse to fish them out, and just as she bent down to retrieve them, Teddy! pushed her into the muddy bog."

"Never mind," he said. "You're definitely good sports and I pronounce you the winners!"

"Oh no they're not!" retorted an angry-looking individual on whom I had never laid eyes before. "I claim the box of chocolates!"

I gathered it was the prize, which I noticed was tightly clasped under the arm of Mr. Price.

"However," she continued in a high pitched voice. "if there's going to be any fuss, I'll gladly share them with you."

After so saying, this miserable-sounding person pushed her mount forward to receive the prize. She opened the box — and was just about to turn around and offer us some, when a shove from behind sent her off balance. If we were too lady-like to argue, not so our mounts. Without so much as a by-your-leave, and without any warning Teddy and Melody pushed their way forward until they were arrayed one on each side of the chocolate-carriers mount. Then, they proceeded to dive their noses straight into the open box and before the startled onlookers (who by this time had arrived upon the scene wet and bedraggled) could say Jack Robinson, those two greedy animals had demolished the whole box, leaving nary a one for their much deserving partners who were perched up aloft in the now, watery sunshine. Our disgruntled adversary gave a snort of contempt, shrugged her shoulders and turned, about to ride away, calling over her shoulder in a loud haughty voice.

"Some animals, like their owners, have no manners, whatsoever!"

Joan and I were so doubled up with laughter that we didn't bother to reply. Do horses laugh?

As I leaned forward to clean up the chocolately dribble from Melody's chin, I thought I detected a lop-sided grin.

Late afternoon saw us weary travellers all. Hacking slowly back along the traffic-free Chelmsford Road. We rode in single file until we crossed the main highway, then trotted out in groups after entering the lane that led to the bridle path.

This path took us through open farmland to the Blackmore Road, passing fields where cows grazed contentedly, where hedges grew wild, and hawthorn bushes made their own gap-less fencing. Bees droned lazily among the blackberry bushes and birds flew out of the trees disturbed by the chink of many bridles and the steady clip-clop rhythm of the pacing horses mingling with the incessant chatter of the riders.

We rode in small groups on the muddy, pot-holed pathway towards the tiny village of Blackmore, which could be approached by four different entries, coming in from different directions.

On that day the narrow roads that converged into the square were quite free from the normal every day activities.

For there were signs placed at the end of each road, saying,

"ROAD CLOSED FOR TODAY
ANNIVERSARY PARTY
IN PROGRESS"

For this was the day of all days. When the villagers, like so many others all over England, were going to forget the weather and all their troubles and enjoy a real lively celebration party.

They had collected and saved money for weeks, by holding dances, bingos and whist drives, and now they were going to let their hair down. They had planned a sing-song and dancing in the square for the evening entertainment and the three landlords of The Bull, The Black Horse and The Leather Bottle were going to provide the drinks — to help the singers along — someone had kindly offered them the use of a piano that stood in place of pride on a flag-bedecked stage, outside the Leather Bottle's front door.

The tables for the late afternoon's tea had been erected and set with paper table cloths of patriotic hues, and set with mugs and plates decorated with cross-flags and a head and shoulder picture of the happy Royal couple, Queen Elizabeth and Prince Philip. These momentous pieces of fine crockery to be saved for posterity were placed at regular intervals on each side of the whole length of the tables, vying for position with cakes, and sandwiches which were piled high as vast mountains, and placed side by side were large bowls of fruit and wobbly jellies.

There was confection in abundance weighing down those groan-laden tables.

You may wonder how I knew all this. Well it was revealed to me .... much later ....

The hard-working inhabitants had toiled all morning preparing for this feast and were only waiting for the jollifications to begin.

Those poor souls!

Were they in for a rude awakening!

Now never let it be said that it was all my fault; blame the wind, the late kit fliers — and the donkeys ....

The latter, poor innocents, who were to give rides to the children after the great feast, tucked away for the time being in the corner of a field behind a high hedge and practically invisible from the main road.

Anyway, just before I reached the duck pond, a kite had left the owner's grasp. This kite was no ordinary run-of-the-mill kind; it was an ugly apparition in the shape of a dragon; from the monster's tail, in rainbow profusion, hung balloons of all shapes and sizes.

This whirling, frenzied object careered down from the sky and found a landing spot — right in the middle of the menagerie of donkeys.

How those terrified creatures escaped in the confusion I never found out, but escape they did, and were running helter-skelter down the road when I had the misfortune to encounter them.

I had a devil of a job to live down what happened next.

You see, I had left the main party of riders to answer an urgent call of nature, probably due to the partaking of so much liquid on the outbound journey. In a hurry, I trotted out smartly to the nearest pub, hoping to remedy the situation and that was how Melody came to find herself joining in with the panic-stricken herd of donkeys.

As one, we all charged into the village square, upsetting tables, scattering revellers, then up onto the stage, and twice around the piano — talk about a carousel without music — the noise from the angry frightened crowd was enough.

Where the other horses were, I had no idea. All I wanted and finally managed was to escape from that place before I was lynched. When the people dispersed — as if by magic, I found a clearing between the instigators of the affray and cantered off post haste.

I would apologize later, that is if anyone ever found out who the guilty party was.

Be sure your sins will find you out ...

Some months later, I received wonderful news: my daughter was expecting her first baby. I was hoping it would be a girl because Maggie had a son in March and I wanted to even up the sexes. As soon as I heard Irene's news I made a list of the gifts that I wanted to buy the new baby.

Bert and I had a conference, we came up with the idea of a super baby buggie.

Irene fell in love with the idea.

"I'd like a Swallow-make pram, mum," she said, "In black and white."

So the first chance I had I made for the baby carriage store which was located thirteen miles from our village, in the Essex town of Ilford. It was quite a busy town with many fine stores and a small market where one could simply browse for ages. There were bargains in ribbons, silken threads and off-cuts of material — a needlewoman's paradise: market stalls sold fresh fruit and vegetables, wet fish and shell fish, and a meat vendor who also displayed fowl and fresh farm eggs. The noise and the bustle of the shoppers and the loud cries of the stall-holders shouting — "What about a bunch of ripe bananas? Look Matey! I just picked 'em myself this morning. Here Missus! now don't go away, I've got some lovely ripe tomatoes! If you don't wa'nna fry 'em, you can always chuck 'em at the old pot and pan."

Now tucked away in the corner of the market was a small cafe where the vendors would sit for a smoke and a chat, a coffee and maybe a snack. The heady aroma of the coffee brewing always lured me to that spot. I would thoroughly enjoy my day of shopping here, it was a place of enchantment for the shop-starved Yokel from the country.

This kind of shopping however, wasn't the real reason for my visit, but how could I resist the temptation once I was there, and I did need some wool, as when I did have the time I was an ardent user of the knitting needles.

So, with the minor purchases made, and the afternoon's weather gloriously sunny, I took a notion to disdain transport and continue to the carriage store afoot.

There it stood in the window! The Pram — the one any mother would be proud to push around.

There was no price tag showing ... but to heck with the price when you're a doting grandparent.

Without further ado I marched into the store and up to the dapper little salesman who beamed with pleasure when I explained about the article I wanted from the window.

"Certainly Madam!" he said. "No trouble at all, I'll have it out of the window in a jiffy. Yes! we do deliver," he told me.

I knew that was the one Irene wanted, the price was right so the sale was quickly concluded, leaving a little time for conversation between the salesman and myself, before I caught my bus back home.

During the course of this conversation the topic of the Queen's anniversary came up.

"Do you know," he said. "I visited my brother that day, I was invited to his street party. It was to have been a splendid affair."

"Oh Yes!" I replied, genuinely interested.

"Where was this?"

"A small village in Essex — Blackmore, actually, I don't suppose you know of it — do you?" he asked me.

I suddenly felt peculiar all over, as he went on with his sad tale.

"Well," he continued, "this here fool of a horsewoman, she wrecked our party and ruined the whole day for us."

I nodded sadly, I could have just sympathized with that nice person, paid him for the pram, bade him good-bye and hastened away. Why did I have to spoil his opinion of me? He had remarked that he thought I made a fine grandmother....

Perhaps I still felt guilty, wanted to clear my conscience, so I confessed all and waited with abated breath for his reactions.

He looked at me with disbelief written all over his face, then a smile appeared at the corner of his mouth, which turned into bubbling, hearty laughter.

"I still don't believe it," was all he said.

Had he scolded me, he might have lost a good sale!

I often wondered if he ever told his brother.

It was a long time before I visited Blackmore Village again.

At the end of the year I had to go into hospital for a hysterectomy operation, so there was no riding for me for a few months; Shirley and Bert did most of the chores.

They say you can't keep a good man down, I suppose that quote can also apply to a woman, so it wasn't too long before I was back in the saddle again.

# Chapter Nineteen

# THE GYPSY

There comes a time during one's life-span, when it feels nice to be wanted or useful, that is, whether it be for family or friend. And there's always a calling or profession that we don't like or understand in this world, but we all have to live and exist.

Such is the calling or profession if you prefer to call it of the wandering, lonely tinker — known as the Gypsy.

The word Gypsy, conjures up a romantic figure for the town dweller, but not so for the land owners or poultry farmers.

These travellers of the lanes and byways plague the countryside in their shabby transports of old cars and trailers. You'll find them entrenched (and very hard to dislodge) wherever a green pasture affords a nesting place for their patched vehicles, along with their menagerie of multi-coloured ponies, donkeys and yelping mongrel dogs.

The occupation, if any of these so called didi-coys, is peg making, wood-cutting, knife-sharpening and rag-totting.

The womenfolk hawk ribbons, laces and bric-a-brac door to door; and sometimes offer to tell your fortune for a palm crossed with silver.

To lack a silver coin or refuse to buy a trinket would bring forth a stream of muttered oaths and curses: with evil tidings thrown in for good measure.

My old acquaintance, Jesse Brown, however, proved to be an exception to the rule. He was a friendly soul, clean, sociable and hardworking. I had never met his wife, but old Jesse, was a well-known figure in the village.

He lived with his wife and family in a snug, white and green painted caravan which nestled beside a copse of beech trees behind the Bentley Golf Course, at the end of Dagwood Lane.

We often rode passed his home on the way back from Brentwood and if Jesse happened to be outside chopping wood he would call out and wave to us.

"Hello Matey's! had a nice ride?" and his wire-haired terrier dog would run alongside the fence, yapping, barking and wagging his tail in friendly greeting.

Come rain or shine, summer or winter, when old Jesse wasn't chopping or selling wood, he could be seen perched up aloft on the high planked seat of his rag-and-bone collecting buggy which was pulled by his black and white, fourteen hand pony.

His gnarled old hands loosely holding the reins, clicking his tongue now and then to coax Danny Boy on to a gentle pace.

The old man was a familiar figure in his black, broad-cloth coat, striped shirt and corduroy trousers, with checkered cap and white silk scarf knotted at the throat, the loose ends tucked away behind his braces.

Once in awhile he would ring a brass-handbell and cry out in a nasal twang.

"Any old rags! Any old rags! The traditional call of the rag totter.

Sometimes at sundown, the old man would walk through the woods surrounding his home and go into the Swan Public House for a refreshing glass of ale.

He'd gossip with a few friends, or watch the local lads play a game of dominoes or darts. I never saw him join in, but he chatted to me occasionally, usually about horses, and his many amusing episodes during his years spent as a traveller on the roads. I would say that at that time, Jesse was in his late sixties, short of stature, slim and wiry, with weather-beaten features and a pair of twinkling blue eyes. He seemed a perfectly healthy man to me. So you can imagine my surprise when I received a telephone call early one morning; It was from the owner of the Blackmore Village garage. I couldn't think for the life of me why he would be calling me — I never drove a car.

"Is it my husband you wish to speak to?" I asked him. "Is it about his car?"

"No! Not to worry," he said reassuringly. "It's really you I want to speak to!"

"You know old Jesse? Well, he was here this morning buying oil and he was suddenly took bad, I don't think it's too serious but I couldn't let him drive in that state, so my wife has taken him home — and the pony and cart are still here!"

"I'm sorry to hear that Jesse is sick," I told him, "but why are you phoning me?"

The caller faltered, as if he wasn't too sure how to answer my question. After a few moments of contemplation, he took the bull by the horns and made an astounding request.

"Ur, Umm! Ahh! ... knowing that you ride horses, I thought ... maybe

— you could drive this weird contraption of Jessie's back to his home. I can't do it — I'm too busy, and besides" he added in a pathetic tone. "I'm scared stiff of horses. I've already given the animal a couple of pounds of carrots hoping to keep it occupied, but he won't stand still. Whatever shall I do?"

I could picture the scene outside his busy place of business, then I got to thinking — remembering the day of donkeys and disaster from a previous visit to that village square. With that in mind I deliberated for awhile, then decided, why not! What the heck! you only die once ....

George at the garage must have thought I'd hung up on him and before I could answer, his panicky voice once again assailed my ear drums.

"Oh no! Would you believe it! He's gone and got himself worked over to my neighbour's lawn now — and he's stomping around!"

"I thought you said he was ill," I cried.

"Not Jesse — you fool" he shouted back. "It's that B,,B...B of a horse I'm referring to."

"Well George," I said. "I'd love to help you out, but how am I going to get there, walk? It's all of three miles, and who's going to take me home, pray? once I've delivered the pony and cart to Jesse's."

"Please don't ask me any more questions?" he pleaded.

"Just say you'll do it and I'll send my wife for you."

"If your wife is going to do all that driving up and down wouldn't it be easier if she took the pony and cart back herself?"

"Don't be daft," he yelled, his voice almost rising to a scream. "She's frightened of horses too. Why do you think I'm asking you?"

"Okay! Okay! Keep your hair on," I replied, "there's no need to be rude; and, if you want the pony to stand still until I get there, I'd advise you to tie him up to something and give him a few more carrots."

It was all very well for George asking me to drive the cart, but I'd never driven a vehicle like that before.

"Easy," you say, "Just try it!" — but not on a narrow-laned highway with deep muddy ditches on either side, for that was the kind of terrain I would have to negotiate.

However, it seemed that I wasn't going to be able to back down, as, true to his word the garage owner's wife was on my doorstep within fifteen minutes, that's how desperate he must have been.

I knew she had arrived as the blast from her car's hooter nearly deafened me.

"You'll have to wait a bit," I called down from the bedroom window. "While I change into my jodhpurs and boots."

"Whatever for?" she yelled back.

"Because," I told her, "I might have to leave the cart there if I can't manage to drive it — and just ride the pony back.

I was still leaning out of the window carrying on this conversation when the milkman appeared and put the milk on the step.

He was just about to go off when I shouted down to him.

"Hey milkman! don't go just yet — I want a word with you" — well, some advice really. "Wait a mo, I'll be down in a jiffy!" I knew that at one time our milkman had made his deliveries by a horse-drawn vehicle, his grandfather still did. Only the old man's cart resembled an ancient Roman Chariot: having been blessed with a vivid imagination I pictured the old man standing up in his chariot covered by a breastplate of shining armour topped by a helmet with magnificent plumage — urging his mount (which was a very small pony) into battle.

When I got to the door the milkman stood there patiently waiting.

"What is it you want to know?" he asked. "Hurry up and spill it, I haven't got all day."

"I want some advice on how to drive a pony and cart," I told him.

"Whatever for?" he asked. "Are you thinking of buying one?"

"Certainly not!" I said. "I only want to know how to drive one." Then I explained what had happened to Jesse.

"Oh I see," he said. "Well, I'll tell you all I know, for what it's worth. Listen carefully!

"The main thing is to keep as close to the centre of the road as possible: and remember, there's far more behind you than just the pony's rump. Take your time and don't worry, as old Danny Boy probably knows his own way home.

But, and this is very important — when you have to stop, for any reason, don't stop him too fast and hold the reins firmly, don't jerk on them or pull them too tight — for if you do and he stops sudden like, he'll back right up to the plank you're sitting on, and you'll do a backward somersault — right in amongst the rags."

Some comic scene must have come into his mind, because he laughed so heartily that he almost dropped the pint of milk he was holding.

I stared at him, mouth open wide in surprise. I had never seen him in such good humour before — and at my expense too ...

"He's only trying to scare you," said my agitated chauffeur, who was nervously fidgeting beside her car door.

"I'm sure you'll be able to cope," she reassured me. "So for Pete's sake lets get going!"

To cut a long story short, we finally got to where the frustrated pony-minder was standing by the pony's head with his arms full of carrots and greenery.

"So you got here at last," he remarked crossly.

"Where do you think you've been?" he said to his wife.

"I've been waiting for her to get ready," she told him.

"Well thank goodness you are here," he said to me apologetically. "Because I'm fast running out of foodstuffs — and patience."

I looked over to where Jesse's pony was munching away quite contentedly. It seemed a shame to take away his heaven-sent meal, but I still had work to do at home, time was pressing on and there was still our own horses food to make up: that's if I ever made it back to Jesse's with the cart still intact.

I didn't want to scare the pony, so I approached him slowly and whispered a few words in his ear.

"Come on old lad! Let's be having you, you don't really need any more of these carrots — do you?"

I eased the dish from under his nose and gave it to the garage proprietor. The pony turned to follow but I firmly took hold of his harness, and pointing to the seat on the car I said.

"I don't know how I'm going to get up there?"

"I'll give you a hand," said an interested bystander, who incidently turned out to be the garage-owners neighbour.

"I'll definitely help you to get that greedy animal out of here anytime, because, if he don't go soon I won't have a blade of grass left standing. Come along woman! make it snappy!" he shouted.

"Okay! Okay! I'm going," I retorted sharply. "I've just been waiting for you to help me up."

With a mighty shove, which nearly sent me right over to the other side of the cart, I knew I had arrived up there. I was lucky to keep my balance. I hastily grabbed hold of the wooden-planked seat and plonked myself down in the centre, then grabbing hold of the unaccustomed reins in my palm-sweated hands, and picking up the whip, I waved it menacingly at the neighbour.

"If you want me to take this contraption away," I said. "You're going the wrong way about it."

"Oh don't go on so," he replied "I was only kidding! Just get cracking!"

I ignored his last remark, I just gathered up the reins and with a clickety-click of the tongue just as I'd seen old Jesse do, I urged Danny Boy on: But old Dan didn't budge! not until I gave him a swift whack across the rump with the whip — that made him walk on.

I eased the pony and cart carefully out of the garage forecourt, passed the "For Sale" signs and out onto the road.

By that time I was feeling rather thirsty and as we drew level with the village pub The Leather Bottle where the doors were wide open for business, I wondered if I should chance stopping for a quick-one?

Then I thought, better not, it simply wouldn't do to be caught drinking and driving whil'st in charge of a rag-and-bone-cart. Besides — if anything untoward happened I might be in need of a strong drink later on: so I reluctantly drove on.

We came to the crossroads and turned right at the village hall, then straight on through, down the Blackmore Road.

"It's a beautiful day and there isn't much traffic." I conveyed this information to the carrot-stuffed pony.

"Good thing it's quiet," I told him. "And" I went on. "I hope you're going to be good and not do anything silly. I'd hate to have any bother while I'm sitting up here. You never know whose about at this time of day and I'd hate to be recognized."

There wasn't even a snort of an answer from Danny, he trotted on oblivious to any of my conversation.

Maybe he was still dreaming of fresh, juicy carrots.

After we had traversed a mile or so down the road I lost all my fears and was beginning to enjoy myself in my new found occupation. Well, the driving part anyway! In no way was I tempted to clang the bell or let forth the odd shout, I couldn't do it as well as Jesse anyway and if I did there was no one about to hear me.

This stretch of the road was absolutely deserted.

How lucky could I get?

Taking a quick peep at my wrist watch I noticed it was two-thirty in the afternoon as I passed the Legion Hall, at Stondon Massey and I still hadn't seen anyone I knew — so far so good.

The next corner I came to before re-crossing the Blackmore Road, I new was going to be tricky, as the road narrowed considerably and it was all uphill. I eased the reins to the left as I turned, thank heaven there were no ditches here, just a few houses with carefully groomed lawns and trim flower beds. Strange to say, we never touched the flowers, but the edge of the lawns that sloped down to the road took a bit of a pounding as the left wheels of the cart took a short-cut across them. It was only the first two front gardens, I pulled the reins to the right before we got to the third.

I was scared to look back in case any angry house-holders was watching, I was fully expecting at any moment to hear someone come out and scream.

I was greatly relieved when we reached the top of the slope, and being no other vehicle in sight, I gave Danny Boy another flick on the rump and he trotted smartly across the road to Outings Lane.

We passed the front garden of the Doctor's surgery (the official sunning spot for Cobber) to go past our own grazing fields.

I was hoping that none of our horses would call out, I didn't relish the thought of Danny going up the path in search of them. But all was quiet.

The next Inn we passed was made in silent protest. The pony couldn't ask for a drink — and I didn't dare.

It must have been just after three o'clock when we entered Gypsy Lane, and so far we hadn't encountered any obstacles.

So I was pleased when we came to this long, winding lane, it was cool, green and shady, there was only one thing wrong with it, there just wasn't enough room for two vehicles to pass each other, no way!

Mounted on a horse you could seek refuge on the grassy bank to make room for a passing car or tractor, but in this contraption I hated to think what I would do.

We were halfway through the lane, no transport seeking passage so far, and I was gaining confidence at every trot. I even sang a few snatches of my favourite songs to entertain my four-legged friend, his ears twitched some and he gave a few snorts. Applause! no I didn't think so, I don't think he even appreciated it.

But somebody did ....

I heard a loud clapping, and suddenly a head, and half a body appeared from over the top of the hedge. I saw a black cap, a sunburned face; a bushy moustache; and a wide mouth, smiling.

"Very nice! Very nice!" Said the half-a-man's voice.

"God," I said. "You scared me stiff.'

"No! I'm not God!" He replied. "I'm just a farm worker taking a few minutes rest from cutting the hedge.

I whoa'ed Danny to stop so that I could speak to the farmhand.

It was a good thing that I did, as coming towards us from the far end of the lane, was an enormous farm tractor.

"Now!" I said to myself, "Whatever am I going to do?"

It came nearer, groaning and rumbling and when the driver saw me he stopped and got down from the cabin.

He came over to me.

"Well 'Me Dear," he said. "What are we going to do now?"

"Just my sentiments," I told him.

"Is there anywhere we can back up?" he asked.

"Not from the way I came," I said.

We were just pondering on what action to take when my recent one-man audience came to our rescue.

"There's a gate further along on the other side," he said. "It leads into the mushroom fields, wait a minute and I'll pop over there and see if I can open it."

He came back a few minutes later. "I've opened it," he said.

"Thanks," said the tractor driver. "I'll be the gentleman and back up, you go ahead!"

"You'll have to" I told him. "I can't turn this thing around. I'm only a learner and there's too many trees in the way, and besides," I continued. "I was warned not to get the pony in a backup position." I explained to the driver about how I may end up in the rags.

He laughed! "I'd very much like to see that." he said. "I could do with a good laugh!"

"Not at me, you're not going to," I told him. I'm late enough already.

After that episode I decided it was time we moved on, fast ...

There were no further incidents thank goodness, and I was thankful for that, we arrived at Jesse's safe and sound.

Mrs. Brown was so pleased, she couldn't thank me enough, she even made me a cup of tea and wanted to hear about my journey.

I told her it was a very long story and I would share the story with her and Jesse when he was fit enough to enjoy a good laugh.

I explained that at the moment I was pressed for time.

She was quite happy about that but she did thank me once again and presented me with a lucky charm bracelet and a basket full of clothes pegs. "Oh! before you go," she said. "Jesse said I was to tell you, he will thank you personally as soon as he is fit: he'll treat you to a drink in the Swan."

Just then George's wife drew up in her car.

"I'm sorry to break in on your conversation," she said. "But I'm in a bit of a hurry, as you know we got all behind with the garage work."

That's a laugh! I thought. What about me, getting all behind with mine. Then I thought — well, you can't be much of a guy if you can't help anyone out in trouble.

But I did hope that I wouldn't have any more problems for a very long time ... but problems were my middle name ...

As I was soon to find out ... because my eldest son who had been divorced for two years — was to marry again.

# Chapter Twenty

# FROSTY

To say at this stage that I'd had my fill of horses and riding, would have been a downright lie, but I was getting older and rheumatism was gradually slowing me down.

What with one thing and another, such as Irene being so far away and so busy looking after her little daughter Julie: and Shirley, who had grown into an exceedingly pretty young woman, and was now courting seriously, left me so busy with other chores that riding had to take second place.

The main problem was Frosty, he was still full of beans and needed to be ridden more often. We did consider selling him at one time, he would have been more suited to a much younger rider, as he still did very well in the show-jumping ring; especially in the indoor arena at Harwood Hall.

It was at one of these shows that Bert happened to run into a business acquaintance who was also a horse fanatic, at least his two daughters were, they were excellent riders and they were always on the look-out for another show-jumping pony.

Bert told me that during their conversation, Mr. Lewis said,

"You've got a marvelous pony there — chum. Have you ever thought of selling him?"

"Funny you should ask," Bert said. "Phil and I were only discussing it the other day. You know he's getting a right handful for Phil these days. Why only last Sunday .... Well, here's Phil now! she'll tell you all about it. I'm sorry I have to go now, it's Frosty's turn to jump. By the way, don't forget to ask her if she wants to sell him."

Andy Lewis and I sat on the top step of the stands outside the arena, and over a cold drink I related to him my latest fiasco on a Sunday afternoon outing on Frosty.

"It was so peaceful and quiet that Sunday afternoon," I told him, "what with everyone being away for the day. Bert and Sylvia had taken Foxy and Lady to a showing class over at High Easter, and my two younger lads had been invited to their brother's house for dinner — so I was all alone.

I did plan to do some writing, but Frosty had other ideas! He wasn't too happy just to stand at the end of the garden and watch me writing — and he didn't want to stand quietly grazing either — and he let me know it!

He paced up and down by the fence, whinnying and snorting, so much so that I couldn't write a word, so in sheer desperation I decided to take him out.

Going into the house I changed, and then into the garage I went, to get his tack, I could hear him carrying on even from there. He made such a racket that in my haste to get out to him I forgot to make myself a drink.

Giving him a lecture about noisy animals and what would happen to him if he didn't shut up — I led him over to the stable, gave him a shove inside then brushed him down with vigour, before I put on his bridle and saddle.

He wouldn't stand still for that. In fact, he was in such a damn hurry to leave, that as I opened the stable door to let him out — we came out in a mad rush together."

Mr. Lewis smiled!

"Yes," he said. "He's a real fireball, and no mistake you can tell by the way he gallops up to the jumps."

"Sorry I interrupted you, do go on."

"Well, I tell you, he was in such a rush to get up the road that as soon as I put my foot in the stirrup, and before I was halfway across his back, he took off: trotting up the street like a mad thing. However I managed to get my other foot in the stirrup and right myself in the saddle and holding him in on a firm rein I shouted, hold it lad! Wait for it! Steady boy, steady! Where's the fire? Now then young fellow-me-lad we're going out for a quiet hack, not a free-for-all race, we're not on the Ongar Gallops now, you know.

"He knew I was mad at him, he puffed in disgust, but he did slow his pace. He's got a terrific fast trot you know Mr. Lewis."

Andy listened with interest, although sometimes his gaze left my face to stray across to the show-ring where I presumed he was watching for his daughter's entry into the ring.

I looked across too, but there was no one there I knew.

"Shall I finish the story later?" I asked my half-attentive listener.

"No! No! certainly not," he said. "I'd like to hear the rest of it now. My girls don't go into the ring until after lunch."

"Okay," I said, "here goes!"

*Phil on Frosty, 1969 Essex, England*

"We had covered at least three miles at a fast walk, he had settled down by then. However, after all that rushing about beforehand I felt quite thirsty and it was rather hot, and I was beginning to sweat buckets! I tried very hard to forget I was thirsty by admiring the scenery. It's very pretty there isn't it? once you pass through Haygreen Lane."

Andy agreed with me. "We came to the big house on the corner just by the edge of the woods. Do you know the one I mean? It has a fine paddock and lush green pasture land. They keep a few hunters there I believe."

"Yes they do," he said. "I know the house, and I've often thought how nice it would be if I could have a closer look at it, and at the horses. I often pass that way when I'm driving the horse trailer."

"You must have noticed the apple trees then, all along by the well trimmed hedge?"

"Well that afternoon the trees were full of fruit, ripe and ready for plucking.

I was in luck as I noticed three large juicy red ones. They had fallen off — and were resting temptingly on the top of the hedge."

I paused in my story to sip on my drink.

"Go on! Go on!" Mr. Lewis said. "I'm all agog!"

"So, being so thirsty and making sure no one was in sight, I decided to try for one.

Getting Frosty in position to get one was another story. I couldn't seem to get it quite right. He would be either too far forward or too far back.

After several attempts and just as I was about to give up, we hit pay dirt!

It seemed just the right moment to reach out! I leaned forward — up and off the saddle ...

Frosty! who was probably fed up with all the unaccustomed maneuvers ... shot forward!

What happened next was so funny — although I didn't laugh at the time, because as I leaned sideways to reach the forbidden fruit, I slipped ...

My face came into sharp contact with the hedge and as my mouth opened in surprise at this sudden jolt it somehow managed to fasten itself over the apple.

It's a wonder it didn't choke me!

Undaunted, I scrambled back into the saddle, then beat a hasty retreat into the woods to enjoy my ill-gotten gains.

I had just raised the apple to my mouth to enjoy the first bite when Frosty stepped on an empty juice can.

He bounded straight up into the air, all four hooves leaving the ground together. I nearly swallowed that apple whole.

Do you know Andy, I promised myself there and then, that I would never go apple scrumping again."

"What happened to the apple?" Andy asked.

"Oh I dropped it!" I told him, "the only enjoyment I got apart from the choking sensation and watery eyes, was a little juice. However, that wasn't to be the end of it."

"There's more to come?" my interested listener said.

"Oh yes! for further on in those same woods I thought I had stumbled across a heinous crime ..."

I was just about to go on with my story when Bert joined us.

"Frosty's just won another first place," he said smiling. "Did you see?"

"No" I said. "You told me to chat to Mr. Lewis, well I did, and I got quite carried away."

"Hasn't she finished the story yet'?

Bert looked at his friend searchingly. Mr. Lewis looked back at him and shook his head.

"What's up?" I asked. "You two look as if you're sharing a secret."

Mr. Lewis blushed and looked a trifle guilty.

"Oh dear! Bert," he said, "I haven't found the heart to ask her yet."

"Ask me what?" I said looking from one to the other, half smiling, half wondering. "Is it to do with Frosty?"

"Yes," Andy said. "And if you promise to finish your story, I'll answer your question."

But Bertie was determined to interrupt.

"Has she told you about the murder bit yet — Andy?"

"Shut up Bert, I'm just coming to that."

"As I was saying, before I was so rudely interrupted ...

There we were all nicely calmed down and collected taking the old trail through the first part of the woods, it was very cool through there, and all I could hear was the scrunching sound of the dead leaves. There was no one else in the wood ... so I thought ...

We crossed the small pathway and entered into the next part of the woods, there wasn't a sound and as we emerged from behind a tall thicket I stopped the pony in his tracks.

Don't ask me why — it was just a feeling. And there a few yards in front of us was a tall man with arms outstretched, carrying what appeared to be a dead body. We followed quietly, at a distance. As the path widened

I could see him more clearly. The body was that of a girl, her stocking clad legs were hanging limply, and her long fair hair hung down swinging at every step.

Oh my god! what had I stumbled on, "Shush Frosty" I whispered, as we slowly followed on.

I wanted to see where he would take or maybe bury her, but it wasn't to be — for just then a disturbed bird flew out from the underbrush right between Frosty's front legs.

What a racket he made as he did his second leap of the day. It must have been fully two feet into the air!

The "corpse" jumped down from the young man's arms with a piercing scream. Then the lovers — for that's what they were — fled the scene, probably never to return.

Boy! was I relieved!

I bet they thought I was a right menace."

"Oh I don't know — I think you're quite brave really. I don't know what I would have done in a situation like that — Run — I guess.

"Now then Andy, what did you want to ask?"

"Well," he said, "I don't think I can at present. I'll leave it to Bert." And with that last remark he said, "Goodbye, see you again soon."

I could hardly wait to get my husband home to unravel the mystery, but he made no further comment and it was not until after we had fed and stabled the horses, that he turned to me and said.

"I suppose you're wondering what Mr. Lewis wanted, aren't you? Well, he wanted to know if we would sell Frosty to him?"

"Why should he think that?" I asked.

"Well," Bert said, "I told him — he was getting too much for you to handle. However, it's entirely up to you whether you sell him or not, as I know how much he means to you."

"Yes dear!" I said. "I know he's a handful, but I would like to keep him just a little while longer, because with all his faults I can't bear to part with him."

"Okay then we'll leave it at that for a while, shall we?" Bert said. "But any more nonsense — and off he goes!"

Frosty did behave himself for a time and I was fortunate enough to find another young rider to exercise him some evenings after school. In exchange, she would muck-out the stables.

Her name was Marion — but she didn't last too long ...

One afternoon whilst waiting to go into the show-ring, she repeatedly tapped him with her riding crop, this must have annoyed him very much. He kicked up his hind legs and delivered her a stunning blow to the hand, which unfortunately broke her wrist.

So it was goodbye — "Marion".

However, as he was still my favourite mount, I just had to ride him again ....

It was a few weeks after my first son got married again, this time to Susan, a divorcee, with three children.

More grandchildren! Plus young Natasha, who was born to them the following May.

It was a Saturday afternoon I recall, and my son and his new family had just gone home.

Frosty was still in the home field, and as it was easier for me to get him rather than Melody — who was in the big fields at Doddinghurst, I decided to take him out.

I tacked him up and mounted him in the field, and Vic my neighbour opened the gate to let us through.

Now at the bottom of my garden just beside the gate, was a tall oak tree, and who should be up there in the thick leafy branches was none other than Vic's large black cat — sleeping, and probably dreaming of a fat juicy mouse, and, at the precise moment I passed under the tree the imaginary mouse must have tried to escape ...

The cat in his dream must have been ready to pounce ...

He let out a series of screeches, and dropped down from the tree right onto Frosty's rear end.

Well, I know how I would jump if a cat's claws suddenly landed on my lap — and poor Frosty — was no exception.

He dashed up the garden and out through the garden gate, as if the devil himself was after him and my knee hit the gatepost with a resounding whack, and I yelled with pain as he galloped up the street heading for the Blackmore Road, I just managed to pull him up at the corner. He was in a real sweat.

I should have turned him around and headed him back there and then, but ever brave or foolish was I, for I allowed him to continue on towards the village of Navestock about three miles on. He was quite calm by the time we reached The William the IV pub, so I ventured a little further afield to the Chequers Arms at Navestock — taking to the grassy verges for a trot and a canter, and when we came to the long stretch of grazing land just before the Chequers Inn, I put him into a gallop.

He went like the wind and jumped the wide ditch in style.

"Okay Lad! Steady there! Steady! That's enough!" but instead of slowing down he continued to gallop on — up to — and right across the publican's front garden. It was a good thing for me that there were no customers there at the time — admiring the floral display, they would have been trampled in the rush, like some of the flowers. I felt like strangling him. Instead, I turned him sharply around, jumped the garden fence, and away we went — galloping back the way we had come.

"Stop! You blighter!" I called out to him, but to no avail, my pleas fell on deaf ears as we headed for the wide ditch again.

I gave a strong tug at the reins just in case he put his head down to throw me, he often did that, and I was taking no chances as we cleared the ditch. A few more tugs on the reins and he finally responded. Out of breath I halted him for a spell.

"Now," I told him. "We'll jolly well walk the rest of the way! We've had enough galloping for one day! I think we'll take a different route back, where there are no grass verges!"

I thought — that would stop him, but he was still full of beans.

All went well until we reached the next stretch of grassy pathway just before the Green Man Inn, where, known to me in one of the cottages close by was a dear little grey donkey.

I thought he was cute, but to Frosty he was a menace, and just as we drew level with the cottage in question, the donkey, who was behind the hedge let off a resounding bray!

"Hee Haw! Hee Haw!-w-w-w!"

That did it ....

And once more — a galloping we did go! well, for a hundred yards or so — then he spotted something unusual in the grass.

I knew what it was — it was an old bicycle tube.

Goodness knows what Frosty thought it was, a snake probably, but whatever he thought it was he didn't like it. Stopping dead in his tracks, down went his head between his front legs — and over the top of his head I went sailing. — CRASH!

I landed flat on my back on a hard piece of stone. I felt the breath leave my body and I was so dazed that as I looked about me — I didn't know which way I had come from — or where I was going ....

A couple from a nearby cottage ran over to help me to my feet. It was a friend, Freddy Parks and his sister.

"You all right Phil?" Freddie asked. "Crickey! you went a cropper, I thought you had broken your back. How are you going to get home?"

"Riding him! of course." I said. "I can't walk all that way."

Freddy stared at me in amazement!

"You're not getting up there again — are you?" he said to me. "You must be mad!"

"Yes! I am getting up there, as you put it, and yes! I am going to ride him — but I assure you — it will be for the very last time!"

"I'm glad to hear it," Fred responded.

Then turning my attention back to Frosty, I picked up the crop and waved it threateningly under his nose.

He blinked and back away, I looked down at my hands to see if I had hurt them and I was surprised to see I was still clutching the reins. I made ready to mount and as I did so I heard Freddy's sister say.

"She's not going to ride him again — is she?"

"She is you know," Freddie replied.

Then looking up at me, she said. "I strongly advise you to make yourself a strong sweet cup of tea as soon as you get home. And" she continued, "if I were you I'd get myself a quieter horse to ride."

"Don't worry," I replied, "I'm going to."

It was then that I finally decided that Frosty would definitely have to go. It was either him or me.

Before I ended up with a broken neck — or worse.

Mr. Lewis was very pleased when we telephoned him to say that at last, Frosty was up for sale.

But I was still sorry to see him go, in spite of all his misdemeanors. He was going to a good home and excellent stables, and from time to time, I visited him in his new home.

He took part in show-jumping events until he was sixteen years old, and my daughter-in-law's brother, David, was his blacksmith — he wrote to tell me the day Frosty died.

I wept buckets — but I did have some wonderful memories of him and the happy and scary times we shared — As for the many photographs, although somewhat faded, I treasure them to this very day — of Frosty and I riding the Kelvedon Range.

# Chapter Twenty-One

# ACCIDENTS WILL HAPPEN

Melody was a likeable character, not a bit like Frosty. Where he was wild, she was calm, serene and very gentle. She wasn't at all keen in taking part in the show-jumping events, she wasn't the type to enter for showing, and as I was too old for the gymkhanas any more we found our pleasures in the simple things in life, such as — long rides into the country, exploring new pathways and short-cuts across the empty fields.

She was a patient animal, ready to stand quietly if I perchanced to meet and chat with another rider.

She would show great interest in the newcomer and never put her ears back or show other signs of aggression. In fact she seemed to welcome these encounters, especially if we stopped beside a local Inn, she seemed to sense, maybe she would get a tray of light ale and a few crisps if I stopped to chat for any length of time. When I had some spare time on my hands I would try out a few steps of dressage, or my feeble attempts at it.

Melody tried very hard to help me with this and I appreciated it, we were so close, she was a one woman mare, and I never ever let anyone else ride her. Bertie once told me — "If you want your horse to do everything you tell it — then just ride it yourself."

However, Melody and I got on so well together I just couldn't believe my luck, but like all creatures great and small there is always a habit or fear they have — which sometimes takes time to discover.

And so it happened to me one Sunday afternoon whilst out in a company of five riders ... destination unknown ...

Someone suggested we ride out to The Gallops near High Ongar.

"Good idea," Bert said. "Let's go by way of Clapgate."

So Bert and Irene, who had played hooky from her domestic chores led the way, and Irene's friend who had recently bought a pony, and was at that time temporarily boarding at our stables, followed, leaving Shirley and I to ride drag .. We collected the others dust and also directed the traffic.

The day was warm and sunny and we took the path through the home wood to School Lane and then turned the horses left to Chivers Lane. We passed Dennis Warren's apple orchard, but I wasn't tempted to scrump for apples, then onto the path that led through Clapgate.

There was a scrap-merchants yard to the fore, where many sheets of metal were stored. "Thank God it's not windy," I said to Shirley. "I'd hate to find out what would happen if that lot clattered down in the wind."

"Why! What do you think Melly would do?" Shirley asked.

"You said she wasn't scared of anything!"

"There's always a first time," I told her.

"Oh look at those Shetland Ponies in Mrs. Watson's field." Irene called over her shoulder. "Aren't they sweet?"

Just then Mrs. Watson came out of her cottage to wave to us as she called out a greeting.

"Where are you all off to?" she asked. "It's all right for some people to have all the fun."

I reined-in Melly to chat for awhile, I wanted to find out a little more about Shetland Ponies. I had thought about buying one for my grandchildren.

We didn't seem to be talking for very long, but by the time we had finished the other riders had disappeared.

Melly didn't appear unduly worried all the time I was talking, but as soon as she realized the other horses had disappeared, she wanted to be off.

"Okay old girl, don't fret. We'll soon catch up with them," I told her. "They couldn't have gone very far. Let's have a trot shall we?" Which we did!

On past the small pond, where my boys used to fish for tiddlers, past the pea-fields, and on toward the little humped-back wooden bridge. I never noticed that it had rotted slightly in the centre, but I think Melly did .... Because — just as she reached the centre — she stopped ...

I still couldn't see what was wrong, so, thinking she was just being awkward, I gave her a tap with the crop. She hesitated! then placing one hoof carefully forward she stepped on the rotten plank. It creaked and groaned as she then put her weight on it. It must have scared her out of her wits, the next thing I knew was we were high in the air as she leapt across the next few feet, that would have been fine .. we were safe and I was still mounted — but, she didn't stop there, oh no! she dashed full pelt across the next few yards of grassland, skidded right, and landed me straight into a large hawthorn tree.

The thorns tore a rent right across the front of my riding cap, into my face, and across my hand as I reached up to ward them off.

There was blood everywhere, on my hands, down my shirt-front and on Melody's neck. I managed to pull her clear of the tree, she must have smelt the blood, because she began to get panicky.

I know I must have screamed, yelled or something, and Bert who couldn't have been too far ahead, must have heard me, for he came galloping back with the others in tow.

I could hear him laughing as he pulled Lady to a halt.

"You don't have to scream because you thought you were lost," he said jokingly.

Then as he drew nearer, he exclaimed. "Good grief! you look like you've been pulled through a hedge backwards, what have you done to your hat?

"Oh dear! Oh dear!" he said with genuine concern, "Whatever have you been up to?"

"What does it look like?" I retorted rather crossly.

I was near to tears!

He drew even closer. "What's happened to your face? I'm sorry I laughed!" he said.

"You've had a fight with a hedge, haven't you?"

"It was that prickly hawthorn," I told him.

"What! That one over there?" he said.

"I can see it — why couldn't you?"

"Don't ask silly questions," I answered him angrily. "And by the way — how did you manage to get over the bridge?" I asked him. "Fly......

"No!" He said. "We went around it. We cut through the hedge and rode around the outer field — and, if you hadn't been so busy chatting, you'd have seen which way we went.

"Never mind — you won't die!" Was all the sympathy I got from him.

"What do you want to do now?" he asked. "Go back?"

We did, but only as far as the Watson House, where after seeing my wounds Mrs. Watson asked me into her home for a quick wash and a thick dab of cold cream to cover the sore spots.

The others waited outside ....

Why did it have to happen to me? .... Don't ask!

However, I did finish the ride without further mishap. My face did clear up eventually without leaving a tell-tale mark.

In fact, the beginning of other events that took place completely erased the whole incident from my mind ...

My son Geoffrey came home late one evening and told me he was going to get married at the end of the month.

"This is rather sudden," I said to him.

"How on earth do you expect me to get a new outfit by then?"

"You'll find a way," he said. "You always do!"

"Yes!" I said. "But I haven't had my holiday yet."

"What holiday?" he asked. "You never mentioned you were going on one." "I don't tell you everything," I said.

To tell the truth, the holiday was at that time only a thought in my mind. Because ....

How long can one go on before the wanderlust takes over? This time I told myself, what about a complete change in travel?

I had crossed the ocean by air, explored the country by horse and car, now, a sudden urge possessed me to take a trip on the ocean.

Brochures I had seen by the score, they had come through the post, or by my own collecting. I could never pass the travel agents in Brentwood without taking two steps back and entering into a wanderers paradise.

The Cunard Line I noticed were doing a speciality, the colourful poster read.

ENJOY CONSTANT SUNSHINE
AND
EIGHT ROMANTIC NIGHTS
COME SAIL WITH US
TO THE CANARYS
ON THE Q.E. 2

The sunshine part was most appealing, as for romance — well, I had my doubts. Although they do say life begins at forty or thereabouts, and — as to what Bertie would say to romance I could only take a guess. Especially as he being a poor sailor would probably refuse to accompany me...

Then of course, there would always be the nagging question of ... who could I con into helping with the horses?

There I was to be in luck. I knew Shirley would soon be taking a holiday, and I made it my first priority to find out when.

With that problem solved, the very next day I put into action "OPERATION SEA CRUISE". Then all I had to do was to try and coax Bertie into parting with the necessary cash.

It was easier than I thought — within a week I had managed to obtain a berth to sail on the next cruise. How!? Somebody had cancelled, Bless E'm! Bert wrote out a cheque, and by the Saturday morning I was packed and ready to go. Shirley and her parents, anxious to see the great liner at close quarters, offered to drive me to Southampton Docks, and so on a glorious May morning we set off.

This was about the time of one of the greatest I.R.A. scares, and the customs officers were as methodical as a monkey looking for fleas on its young, and by the time we arrived the customs sheds were crowded and there were policemen everywhere.

A stern-looking officer with an over-sized Alsatian dog stopped us, just outside the customs barrier.

"I'm sorry," he said, as he barred our way.

"Only passengers are allowed past this point, visitors must remain behind the barrier. You can say your goodbyes from there."

My friends were so upset, they had driven me all that way only to be turned away at the end. To them, it must have felt like going away on a picnic without any sandwiches.

They were not the only ones! You could hear the "Oohs! and Aahs!" from all quarters and the cries of "Shame! Shame! What is this country coming to, when you can't see your own ships?"

"Now quiet there please, rules is rules," said the policeman.

"I'm only carrying out orders, and it is for the passengers own safety." But Shirley's Dad had to say a few words to the officer on duty.

"I ask you," he said. "Do I look like an Irish saboteur?"

"No," the officer told him. "You look more like a pirate off the Spanish Main, with your dark eyes and tanned skin."

The family laughed at his attempt at what they considered was a feeble joke, especially in the circumstances, and they were still disappointed as they waved their last goodbyes and walked sadly away. Then I was left to my own devices ...

I gazed about me for a bit, searching for someone who appeared as a well-seasoned traveller. I was hoping to pick up some useful information on what cruising on the ocean waves was all about.

I spotted a middle-aged couple who seemed quite friendly, they were laughing and chatting together, their luggage resting beside the gentleman's feet. One of the suitcases was so large it was almost as big as a seaman's trunk. I could hazard a guess as to whom that belonged. I was sure it was his wife's, women usually take more luggage than they need.

I was just about to go over to speak with them when a series of piercing shrieks that nearly deafened me came over on the customs Tannoy and a man's voice which I familiarized with a railway station announcer called out a list of instructions, so blaring and garbled that they sounded something like this.

"Hall passengers hembarking at this po-or-nt, please ma-ak your way towar-aw-ds the custom-mm-ta-ab-les, have your tickets-sss and passports-zzz ready."

The unseen speaker repeated this request several times, each one no clearer than the one before. The noise and the confusion ensued for some time, however, the couple who had claimed my previous attention seemed to ignore the announcements, they appeared to be arguing.

"Nay, Nancy lass!" I heard him say in his broad Lancashire accent. "I'll take the big case, you know you can't lift it!"

"But George luvee" she said. "You know I don't trust you with my things, you may leave em behind somewhere."

Fat chance! I thought, he'd have to be blind to leave a case that size behind.

Anyway, George being a dutiful husband picked up the large case, his wife following, and I followed close on their heels. As they approached the customs counters they were split up, Nancy to the left and George to the right, I was given the signal to stand behind him, and the following incident occurred ...

With a terrific struggle George managed to hoist the trunklike piece of luggage onto the counter and the tall young custom's official who stood on duty behind the counter, said to him jokingly.

"My! My! What's this we have here, Long John Silver's Trunk? My word! it's a size, how long were you planning to be away for? I'm glad I'm not the one to be lugging it around."

He looked at poor perspiring George with interest.

"Now, what do we have in here then? Open it up and let's see what's inside."

George did as he was asked, but, in his nervous haste to undo the trunk, it accidentally lurched forward spilling its entire contents of assorted feminine garments in profound confusion all over the table.

The officer stared at George in disbelief! George's face turned scarlet, some of the other passengers tittered as they craned their necks towards where the unfortunate George was standing, to see what all the commotion was about.

"Oh dear! dear! dear! what's all this," the official continued. "Are you the female impersonator attached to the entertainment crowd?" The officer had a job to keep a straight face.

"Certainly not!" George cried in dismay. "They don't belong to me!" he said.

The young man smiled as he looked George straight in the eye, and in a loud voice, he shouted. "They all say that! Okay old son, you can go! Anyone who wears nice underwear like that can hardly be mistaken for a member of the terrorist squad."

He was still laughing as I approached the counter.

He opened my case and glanced quickly through, then seeing my riding trousers and boots, (well, one never knows where one might find a horse to ride) he said. "Oh! And I suppose you'll be telling me you're Lester Pigott in disguise."

"Ha! Ha! Very funny," I retorted.

"It won't be very funny," he said, "if the Captain catches you riding up and down the decks. Okay! you can go. You'll find a steward over there by "B" door waiting to take your luggage aboard. Bon Voyage!"

I was glad to see the back of him, the steward seemed a much nicer man, and as I followed him on to the quayside I stopped for a moment to gaze up in wonder at the greatest Liner in the world.

For there she stood in magnificent splendour, towering above me, her white-painted sides glistening in the afternoon's sunshine, her top decks awash with flags and buntings of many colours dancing and flapping in the breeze.

It was a sight that I had always dreamed about, but had never expected to see, and to think that I was going to step aboard this luxurious floating hotel made my head spin.

I followed the steward up the covered gangway which had been specially decorated for this momentous occasion.

The walls along the red-carpeted corridors were covered in scarlet. On one side a golden lion head adorned by a golden crown stood upon his hind legs as if dancing, and in his front paws he carried a sphere of the world. And on the other side, the scarlet wall was bedecked by The Union Jack, and beneath it a ship's buoy with a message around it to welcome the passengers aboard.

"QUEEN ELIZABETH 2
SOUTHAMPTON
10TH ANNIVERSARY"

I couldn't have chosen a better time for my trip.

It would take pages and pages to describe that holiday in detail, but it was fine to say, I had a whale of a time! Even to winning a bottle of champagne for jiving with a ship's steward.

I had dinner at the Captain's table — then I got lost after the dance trying to find my cabin. I was nearly blown overboard whilst exploring the bow area on the top deck. I ployed quoits and bridge, and danced every evening — and I enjoyed all three excursions on the mainland of the Grand Canary Islands.

Not one horse did I see throughout the entire trip.

At last I could say I had been to sea. Not in it, thank goodness. Although some years after I did explore the depths in a midget submarine.

Now like all good things holidays do have to end, and the time for disembarking soon came around, but even in this I was to have another adventure.

We landed on a Sunday, slightly sad and a little weary, and what followed made me mad — and more weary still!

Docks are drab places for the returning traveller, and on this Sunday afternoon they seemed more so, especially after all that past glamour. There were few porters about to take care of our luggage, and once passed the customs we were complete ignored.

There were three of us that afternoon, last out through the customs, two older ladies and myself. One was an American lady, who had her holiday ruined by falling down some deck stairs during the trip, she had broken her arm, and was still in pain.

"You stand there ladies and I'll see if I can find a porter." I said to them. "There must be one left on duty — somewhere."

After a great deal of searching I did manage to find one, and he followed me back to where my fellow passengers were waiting.

"Let's see how much luggage you have?" he said.

"Oh I think we can manage with just one trolley," and he went off to fetch one.

Duly loaded, we all followed behind him to the lift.

After depositing our cases, (of which there were about a dozen) in the lift, and probably, displeased with the tip — he promptly left us.

Once we were inside, it was a very tight squeeze — and the American woman was still grumbling, which didn't help matters any. We started to ascend, when suddenly the lift gave a violent jerk, it squeaked, jangled and jolted, then stopped altogether between two floors...

Panic reigned as the two old ladies landed on their bottoms on the lift floor, one old dear had her hat down over her eyes and her nose and chin were firmly wedged between two suitcases.

She screamed and struggled as I tried to help her to her feet. The

American, just moaned pitifully and prayed to Jehovah. I tried to calm them down.

"Shush! Shush!" I said. "Do try to be quiet. I'm going to shout for help. Don't panic!" I told them. "It's an open lift and we have plenty of fresh air." The last remark of mine seemed to do the trick, they sat quietly while I, in my ex-army voice yelled ... "Help! Help!" Getting no reply I shouted. "Is there anybody there?"

Good thing it wasn't dark, we could have been mistaken for three crones at a seance. I did think on those lines myself, and I tried hard not to laugh as the lady who had caught her nose in the cases started to cry, which made her nose even redder.

"Please won't somebody help?" I yelled again and again.

After a few more yells and just as I was about to give up from complete exhaustion a voice from above called down the vent ...

"Is there anybody down there?"

"Yes," I said sarcastically, "Three Blind Mice."

"Oh dear," said the invisible man, "what are you doing down there?"

"Waiting for the cat to come and get us," I told him.

"We're stuck in the lift, what else would we be doing, for goodness sake do something! One of the ladies is quite ill!"

"Okay!" said the voice. "I'll be back in a minute but I don't know what I can do, we don't get paid for overtime, especially on Sunday."

"That's charming," I said.

"You — whip-it-quick back here — with help or I'll"...

I never finished the sentence — for just then the lift gave a terrific jolt and up we went.

How it happened I never figured out, perhaps my threatening manner and shouting scared the lift into action, it certainly wasn't any human hands.

As we reached the next floor a bespectacled railway porter stood outside the lift gate, he slid back the door and we tumbled out, it was then I knew how a coal miner must feel when released from the shaft cage...

When I regained my composure I had a few unkind words to say about Dockers, Porters and the like. However, I did thank our rescuer and tipped him handsomely after he helped us all to get our luggage to the train.

And was I ever glad when I saw my son and his wife at the station barrier waiting to drive me home.

I told them about the last few hours, they were very sympathetic, and when I told them about the champagne, they said.

"That's good! Now we have something to celebrate with."
"What's that?" I asked them.
"Why! Geoffrey he's getting married next week."
And what a fiasco that turned out to be .....

# Chapter Twenty-Two

# COACH AND PAIR

I love weddings, especially the dancing afterwards, and at this wedding I never had any young ones to get ready, or to keep clean.

I remembered Carl's wedding when I made the three younger boys sit for ages in the bath tub until it was almost time to go.

They were perfectly clean and also the pinkest guests there.

At this affair I had only myself to dress, although I did have a mad rush on my hands trying to find a suitable gown and matching accessories. The dress was a tight fit mind you, because I hadn't given a thought to my figure over the past week or so. I had been too busy consuming such wonderful food. The dress was rather tummy hugging, but never mind, I could get around that problem easily enough. During the photographic session I could hold my largest purse well to the fore, that should do the trick, then perhaps my middle-aged bulges wouldn't show. Anyway, who was going to look at me, when there would be such a pretty bride around.

I hadn't known Susan very long, all I did know was that she was an ex-beauty queen, and her parents were extremely rich, so and, as she, no doubt was bent on pleasing her in-laws, both she and her family had gone to great trouble and expense to hire a horse-drawn vehicle for the bridal carriage.

I thought it was rather nice of them, but what Bert didn't like about the whole affair was the fact that he had to dress in what he termed it as — a monkey suit — top hat and tails.

He said he didn't feel comfortable in it and I knew why, he isn't that kind of a guy, but Geoffrey who was tall and slender, it suited him perfectly, he looked handsome and debonair.

However, we were both pleased about the coach and pair — that was until we saw it ...

Bert and I drove to the church with Geoffrey, Ray, and Geoff's best man. The rest of the family were to meet us there.

It was the church of St. Peter, a very old and stately building that stood on the top of a hill overlooking the lush, green pastureland of the village of South Weald.

When we arrived, the church was beginning to fill up with the families and friends of the bride and groom, and the fragrance of the many flowers that decorated the aisles and the altar was as heady as summer wine.

As the groom's family, we sat behind Geoff occupying the first three rows of pews, and as we waited for the bride to arrive, I knelt quietly down beside my husband to say a few words of thanks for the wonderful life we shared. I thought about the other children's weddings and the grandchildren we had been blessed with. There were nine of them now, and Maggie was expecting her second child in June. How many more grandchildren would I have?

I thought of all the Christmas presents I would have to buy and the birthdays I would have to remember. Then I got to thinking, I wondered if they would love horses — the way I did. If so, then how many ponies could we afford to buy.

In the midst of my silent reverie I was suddenly aware that a sudden hush had descended upon the congregation, so I opened my eyes then rose to my feet to join the others as the church organ began to play the first triumphant chords of the wedding march.

It brought my mind back into the church — and why we were there...

The congregation turned as one, as down the aisle on her father's arm came the bride — A vision of beauty, in a crinoline gown of white French lace, carrying a bouquet of deep red roses.

I cried during the ceremony as all mothers do.

"There goes another son," I whispered to Bert.

"And you have another daughter-in-law," he said with a smile. "How many do we have now?" he asked me.

"Five," I replied. "So far ...."

The service was sweet, short and simple, the couple exchanged vows and then there were hymns and when they left the altar steps to go to the vestry, we the parents followed to sign as witnesses. There was kissing, handshaking, cheerful patter and good wishes extended to the happy pair before we adjourned to the church arbour for photographs.

It was a beautiful sunny afternoon, not a cloud marred the horizon — so far!

The photographic session went on for some time and whilst the bride and groom were posing, Bert and I slipped out through the church gate to take a closer look at the horse-drawn carriage.

The horses were dapple grey, well groomed and smartly turned out as were the two footmen in their fine grey livery, but, as Bert commented, "they're a badly matched pair — those horses!"

I could plainly see what he meant ...

The colour was fine — but the unevenly matched height of the horses was ridiculous.

"Whoever matched those two horses together wants his head examined." he declared. "One wrong move and I'll warrant there'll be trouble."

"Oh don't say that," I said. "It's unlucky to think that way."

"You mark my words," he said. "I don't like it."

How right his words turned out to be ...

I patted the horses and thought no more about it as we made our way back for the rest of the picture taking.

We were just in time for the last group picture and everyone milled around to watch.

Then there was great excitement as the bride and groom left the church in their carriage on their way to the wedding breakfast amid a show of rose petals, rice and confetti, with the guests cheerfully waving them goody-bye.

A stream of cars gradually passed them as they made their way to Ye Olde Logge restaurant on Shenfield Common to where a sumptuous meal awaited them.

Everyone was seated and the champagne flowed, the meal was ready to be served — but where were the happy couple?

Some time passed, and still there was no sign of them.

There were the usual cheeky comments, the sly looks and the giggles, but after an hour had elapsed it wasn't funny anymore.

The bride's father sent out a search party for them, they returned with a policeman. Susan's Dad took the stage in the restaurant as he tried to explain.

"Not to worry folks," he said, "there's been a slight accident. Geoff and Sue are fine and they'll be with us soon."

The bridal couple appeared about ten minutes later, flushed and a trifle disheveled trying hard to make a joke out of the whole thing.

We were told about the drama later, when the meal was over and the last toast made.

The carriage had just reached the bridge on Weald Road when the larger horse of the two reared up, put his back feet over the traces causing the vehicle to collapse. The co-driver who went to the aid of the frightened couple was brutally kicked by the other panic-stricken horse, breaking the driver's leg. When the police arrived on the scene they sent the driver to hospital, righted the carriage and commandeered a white Rolls-Royce to speed the couple on their way.

"Well," said the bride's new father-in-law, after he had toasted the bride for the umpteenth time.

"If you ever want a carriage wedding again, come to me for advice about the horses!"

"Don't say that," I told him.

"Say what?" he said.

"Why! about marrying again."

How right he proved to be ... Once again... There was to be another Mrs. Holden in the not too distant future and from Bertie's own country at that.

"It's a funny old world," I said to him later that evening. "Here we have six daughters-in-law and not a horsey one amongst them..."

Perhaps it was just as well, as we were told that the open grazing fields behind us that we had enjoyed for many years, were to be sold to a housing developer, so, at the end of the year, and finding that no other adults in the family were really interested in riding we decided to sell Lady Jane to Diane.

Diane loved her and had been very keen to buy her from the very start, and as she was going to leave her job in the city pretty soon and live on a small farm in the country, we couldn't have been more pleased when they both went off together to a new start.

We did see Lady once more, it was a short time after Diane had her mated and put into foal, after that all traces of Diane and Lady vanished from the show-jumping world.

But there, life was full of surprises as it was with shows and show-jumping. You win some you lose some, and so it was with the horses we owned.

There were hangers on wherever all good ponies and horses are.

There were the willing girls who were only too eager too look after the animals as well as the glory of winning a trophy in the show-ring. There was also the petty rivalry between some of the younger girls, but all in all I must be fair, most of them showed a genuine interest in the horse's welfare, and they were kind helpful and friendly, and we got along just fine.

However, the finest example was Shirley. Never a day passed winter or summer, than she put her whole heart and soul into the horses welfare. Whether it was fixing their food, exercising them, mucking-out stables or mending fences, with never a complaining word ... There might have been the odd cuss or two I'll grant you, but it soon passed. Her deep devotion to Cobber was an inspiration to us all, and when Cobber died of old age a year after Shirley moved away, I went to see his resting place in her back garden. The epitaph read.

"TO OUR DEAR COBBER"
"COMRADE AND FRIEND"

I knew how she felt when we just had Melody and Foxy left.

After Lady had gone Bert didn't seem to have the same interest anymore, only when the grandchildren came. Then he took delight in trying to teach our second eldest granddaughter to jump the ditches on Foxy in the big fields behind Blackmore House, where I had first learned to ride many years before.

Without Shirley to accompany me every day and my friend Joan moving away, life seemed so boring and tame, just being able to ride on Sundays. I became so browned off I went out to look for a job. It was in an engineering factory.

I had never worked in a factory before, I hated that kind of noise, it was one of the main reasons I joined the army, because I didn't fancy working in a noisy munitions factory.

I never actually made anything in this new job, I just had to check on how long it took the engineers to make it.

I was what they called a costing clerk.

Even in that job I couldn't get away from animals. Well, not exactly, as my part-time helper was a keeper of donkeys and goats.

She told me of their antics and habits every morning. It was rather difficult for me to concentrate on my hours, minutes, and deducted breaktimes, and as I was silly enough to tell her how much I liked animals, I had to listen to her mating stories in general. I would dearly have loved to cap her stories with one of my own, but once started — the workers would be one up on me with their output .... And I thought, if she knew I was experienced in such matters she might ask me for help. And on the subject of Billys, Kids and Nannys, I didn't want to know. Not even the memories....

All things taken into consideration — I enjoyed my work.

However, even the thoughts of another holiday in Canada that October — with spouse this time, couldn't dampen my ardour or the yearning for a good horse under me, and to be able to ride for miles and miles — All day and every day.

So when my goat friend and colleague happened to say to me one day. "Why don't you try a riding holiday in the New Forest?"

I thought — well that's an idea, why didn't I think of that?

"There's a brochure in the Horse and Hounds Magazine," she said. "And I don't think it's too expensive."

"We take that magazine at home." I told her. "I'll scan it this evening. Thanks for the idea!"

"You're welcome," she said. "And if it's okay, let me know. I wouldn't mind going myself."

"Why, do you reckon they keep donkeys?" I asked mischievously.

"Don't be cheeky," she replied, her brown eyes full of laughter. "I can ride horses too," she said. "Even though I don't own one."

"We had best get on with our work," I told her. "Here comes the boss!"

But for the rest of that day, my mind mulled over as to what she had said, then as usual, I started to scheme.

How! — I had yet to figure out.

With me the word maybe, never entered into it.

# Chapter Twenty-Three

# HORSEY HOLIDAY

It was the year nineteen-eighty-two and I was fifty-seven years old — old enough to know better and to take life easier, but no! On a Saturday afternoon in the middle of July, England's rainiest season, I played hookey from work, and with the aid of my son Anthony — who came to my rescue once again — this time accompanied by his wife and their two children, we journeyed by car to the Wood End Stables in the New Forest of Hampshire.

"Let's see what mischief you can get up to there?" Anthony said as he turned to me and winked his eye.

"Ah! don't you wish you were staying with me?" I asked him.

"We do Nan!" two voices piped up from the back seat.

"When you get bigger," I told them. "Then no doubt you'll want to come on your own."

After that the children were very quiet and the rest of the journey passed uneventfully — until we came to the last lap...

"Where the dickens is it?" Anthony said, "Have a look at the map again, Mother! Are you sure it's on this road?"

"That's what the lady told me over the telephone," I told him.

"Women! and their sense of direction," he grumbled.

"Stop and ask someone," Pat ventured to say.

"Not likely!" Anthony told her. "Do you think I'm going to keep stopping the car for that? We'll go back to the last crossroads and try again from there."

And so we did, but to no avail, but as he slowed down I made a dive for the window yelling out to a bunch of football fans going by.

"We're lost! Can you tell us where the Wood End Stables are?"

I thought Anthony was going to shoot me, but I was glad I called. Not only did one of the fans know of it, but he proceeded to tell me its history, he might have done just that, but his friends stopped his oration, calling out to him.

"Hurry up Tom! We'll be late for the match.

With Tom's instructions fresh in his mind, Anthony soon found the place we were looking for — And what a place it was ...

Dump! Would have been a better description.

At first glance it reminded me of the Goat Yard, without the goats. The ground was muddy and covered with whisps of straw, the house looked so ramshackled I expected any minute to see it come tumbling down. Pat and Anthony looked at it in disgust.

"You're not staying there, Mum," they said.

And I felt the same way. I was so disappointed especially after coming all that way.

We were just about to turn around and go back the way we came, when a blonde slim young woman in riding trousers came out of the house and made her way towards us.

"Hello there!" she called. "Are you the lady who is going to spend a week with us?"

She stared straight at me through the open car window and I didn't know what to say. Then on a sudden impulse I jumped out of the car to shake her hand. "Sure," I said. "Why not!" as I thought to myself, I'd seen and stayed in worse places than this during my years in the service.

She beamed at me, "That's the spirit," she said, taking my large suitcase that my son had reluctantly removed from the back of his car.

"Ow! look at all those ponies!" young Anthony shouted. "Can I have a ride Dad? Please! Dad."

The young lady who evidently was the owner of the stables introduced herself as Barbara.

"What a dear little boy!" she said to me. "Is he your grandson?"

"Yes" I replied, "and he's madly keen on ponies."

" My Nans got two horses," he told her with pride, not to be left out of the conversation, in case they forgot his request for a ride.

"The lady is busy son," Pat said trying to keep her son in the car and then, as if to clinch the matter a small boy came riding towards us on a miniature forest pony.

"Mother!" he called. "Mother! is that little boy going to stay with us?"

"I'm afraid not," she told him, "but while he's here will you let him ride your pony?"

And so it was that as Barbara and I talked and walked together towards the house — my grandchildren rode that little pony twice around the house and in the front paddock.

"You come with me," Barbara said, "and I'll show you to your room, it's at the back of the house just across the yard, it's the annex and it's usually reserved for seniors.

Oh dear! I thought, she's twigged I'm ancient, I think she must have read my thoughts or noticed my crestfallen expression, because she righted her statement by saying.

"I keep the younger visitors by me in the house where I can keep an eye on them."

"Very wise." I told her. My son, who had followed us over turned to my hostess and said.

"Don't be too sure it's the children who need watching, I know of some seniors that can get up to all sorts of tricks, especially on horses!" The last part of his statement fell on deaf ears as my hostess was well to the fore by then, taking long manly strides to the annex. We followed, but once inside when I climbed the stairs, Anthony stayed below.

It was then that I noticed that Barbara still had her boots on, she didn't seem to worry about the mud on her carpet. At the top of the stairs she hurried along the white-painted corridor until she almost reached the end, here she paused pointing out to me two doors.

"That's the bathroom and that's the toilet," she said. "And your room is at the end Number 13, she dropped my case by the stout-oak door, inserted a large brass key into the lock, turned it and pushed open the door. She stepped inside — and I followed her in ...

I looked about me in surprise, it was a beautiful room. The walls had been painted in a deep shade of pink and at the two Tudor latticed windows hung chintz curtains of a lighter hue, and the large double oak-headboard bed was covered by a quilt embroidered with cream silk roses, very pretty, and it looked jolly comfortable too. The floor that was wood-stained and polished, had a small fringed rug on either side of the bed, there was also a small chair in the room, a desk, a wardrobe and an old-fashioned wash-stand complete with a china hand basin and jug. It all looked very cosy and I was beginning to feel happier by the minute.

It was then that I heard my son talking to someone in the hall below, I thought he should see this room, then he would go away feeling much easier in his mind, so I turned to Barbara and said. "My son's downstairs! Is it okay if he comes up for a minute?"

"That's fine," she said. "He can stay as long as he likes, but you will have to excuse me, I have other visitors arriving shortly; and I still have the evening meal to supervise. You freshen up if you like, then come over to the house for supper — It's at eight o'clock," she called out as she passed Anthony on the stairs. "And by the way," she said as an afterthought, "there's no need to lock your door, there are two other visitors staying in the building. Two nice lads, so you have no need to feel nervous." I called out my thanks, and, with a "see you at eight," I turned to welcome Anthony into my new quarters.

Mm! Mm! this looks all right! Do you want to stay now?"

I smiled as I nodded my head.

"Okay then, he said. "As soon as I've detached my offsprings from the ponies we'll be on our way. I'd like to get the children home before dark."

Yes! I thought, and before the football results are over.

"Thanks again son," I said, "and tell your father, I'll phone him tomorrow night, say good-bye to Pat and the children for me." And with that parting shot Anthony was off and away, leaving me to tackle my unpacking.

The bridle and saddle I had brought with me I hung over the chair, I put my clothes into the wardrobe and found a place for the rest of my knick-knacks — then I went to the bathroom for a refreshing shower. I should have taken a short nap really, but, not wanting to lose a precious minute I dressed hurriedly and went outside to take a walk-about, to explore my new surroundings before the light failed ....

The house didn't look so bad now after a closer inspection. It was very old, probably it had been a country seat of some Lord of The Manor during the Tudor Period. I was no expert on those matters, but what I did like about it was the thatched roof with the two tall chimneys, the small gabled-latticed windows that glowed a fiery red from the last rays of the setting sun.

I made up my mind I was going to like it here.

As I wandered over to the first section of stables and made friends with a fifteen-hand liver-chestnut mare, I knew I had done the right thing by staying.

It was getting dark when I retraced my footsteps back to the house, the door stood slightly ajar and as I pushed it open to step down into the warm dining room, a wonderful smell arose from the freshly baked batch of bread and the heady aroma of fresh percolated coffee.

Those delicious smells suddenly made me realize I was hungry and that I hadn't had a meal since noon.

Barbara bid me welcome and seated me down to supper at the centre table to join a dozen or so other guests who were later introduced to me over coffee. They were a jolly bunch, the visitors and the stable hands who joined us by the open fireplace for coffee, to where a cheerful log fire burned in the open grate.

When her busy days work was finished, Barbara came over to sit with us as we discussed the week's programme, the places of interest we could visit, as well as the riding events.

The remainder of the evening was passed in pleasant conversation mainly about horses, naturally! but it was nice to be with so many people who shared the same interests.

Time marched on, I could see everyone was beginning to feel sleepy by their sighs and yawns and I was no exception. I was ready to hit the hay! so saying goodnight to my fellow riders I left for the annex and a good night's rest — or so I hoped...

I still hadn't seen the two young persons who were to be my fellow boarders in the annex so I presumed they were already in bed, so going to the bathroom before retiring, I tiptoed along the hall trying to be as quiet as a mouse, and not a soul stirred as I made my way back to my bed. I didn't need any rocking for as soon as my head touched the pillow I must have dropped off to sleep.

Sometime during the night I was awakened by the sound of soft footfalls, perhaps it's the lads returning, I said to myself, but once awoken from my slumber I needed a glass of water and a visit to the little girls room, so I got out of bed, slipped on my dressing gown, picked up a glass from the wash stand and made for the bedroom door. I turned the knob and pulled — no response — I tried again, harder this time — still nothing happened. I went back for the key, turned it in the lock — still nothing happened, it wouldn't budge.

Now although the water wasn't all that important and neither was the call of nature, I could have waited until morning, but I had this sudden urge to get out of that room. Claustrophobia? — maybe or the thought of being trapped should there be a fire.

Whatever it was, I panicked!

There was no chance I could get out by the window, they were much too small, even smaller than the ones at the front and they were half covered by the thatched eaves, so, back to the door I went, and proceeded to give it a series of bangs with my clenched fists, this procedure proved very painful so I picked up my riding boot and whacked the door with that.

After what seemed like an eternity but was probably only a few minutes I heard the sound of running feet along the corridor, then a man's voice, shouting outside my room.

"What's wrong number 13?"

"Oh thank goodness someone's there," I called back. "I'm locked in!"

"Haven't you got a key?" the voice asked.

"Yes" I said. "But it won't turn, and I didn't lock it anyway."

"Don't upset yourself," the voice continued. "I'll get some help."

I sat by the bed and waited and waited, by this time I did need the bathroom! It must have been a good half-hour or so before I heard footsteps again, this time there were more voices, the deeper tones of a man and Barbara's excited high-pitched voice.

"She's in here," I heard her say. "In number 13."

I hadn't thought about the number until then, then I began to wonder. It was supposed to be unlucky!

Oh well! I might have guessed it would be unlucky for me ...

"Now when I turn the knob, we all push together," the deeper voice of command began. "And if that don't work I'll just have to force the lock."

"Stand clear Phil," Barbara said, "And we'll have you out in a jiffy."

I never answered, only prayed. I expected to see the battering-ram forces bursting in at any minute, but after a few heave ho's! the door remained intact. It was then treated to an assault from a jemmy and hammer — the pounding lasted about ten minutes, and finally with a swift lunge at it by the caretaker's heavy shoulders the door swung back with a crash — and in came my four rescuers.

As soon as I was calm and collected I thanked them all and apologized for all the trouble I had caused, as I explained to them, I had never locked myself in a room, ever, I was too scared there might be a fire, when I shut the door, it must have locked itself automatically.

"Yes" Barbara said. "The lock must have jammed, never mind, try to go back to sleep and the caretaker will fix it in the morning."

Well, after all that excitement in the middle of the night, I was so tired that as soon as my head touched the pillow I must have gone straight back to sleep.

Unfortunately for me, that little episode wasn't to be the last of my unhappy experiences, because, the next morning right after breakfast I was extremely sick with stomach cramps, which lasted throughout the day and while the others were enjoying themselves on a whole days trek into the forest I was confined to bed. My sickness didn't last too long however, by the time they returned I felt much better and was able to join them for supper and listen with envy to their fantastic tales.

Later that evening, Barbara called me over and said how sorry she was that I had been indisposed.

"I'll make it up to you somehow," she said. "Do you think you could stay another two days? At no extra charge of course."

I agreed! And the rest of my holiday went off without a hitch.

My rides into the forest with one of the guides or a group of riders were something I shall never forget, especially when I was put in charge of the week-end riders. Now that was a laugh!

There were the stragglers. The one's who knew it all. The clever one's who tried to ride up the highest slopes, and were too scared to come down, and the ones who were supposed to be experienced riders, who kicked the sides of their mount to urge them on and at the same time pulled back hard on the reins. I tried to explain what would happen — but — so after a few of them became un-seated by the horse's instinctive reactions, they realized I knew what I was talking about.

The best part of riding in The New Forest was the absence of traffic, for once in the fields and on the moorland heath we could ride undisturbed — the only time we did perchance to meet a vehicle was when we reined-in at the Inn for our meals.

Our parking problem was solved as we were allowed to stable our mounts in the farmer's cattle stalls, which were only a few yards away and always vacant except on market days; whereas, the motorist would have some distance to go to park their cars before sitting down to a meal.

Then together, rider and motorist would sit and watch the deer and wild moorland ponies come close to the tables to beg for scraps.

Sometimes we rode out late into the evening, and it would be almost dark as we made our way back, riding in the half-twilight. Up hill and down wooded slopes passing close to rows of fir trees and hearing the sighing of the wind whispering through the pine needles or the soft patter of a late evening's shower descending on the springy turf.

Splashing through the shallow waters of a stream, to see the water rats scuttling to their homes along the muddy banks.

The night owl's call, "To Whit! Too Woo!" and the furry, silent creatures of the forest scurrying home beneath the horse's feet. The sound of nature's wild life never seemed to distract the horses, or the darkness their sense of direction.

I'm sure they could have found their way home alone, or blindfolded for that matter.

These were not the only delights that I experienced on that glorious week's holiday.

One morning as it was much too hot to ride, Barbara craftily asked me if I would like to go to the beach for the day.

"I'll take you," she said. "If you'll look after my young son for the day, he's quite fond of you!"

I agreed, as I quite liked the idea, and so did young Tim.

He soon had his bucket and spade and his swimming trunks ready, along with his pop, potato-chips and sandwiches.

We had a wonderful day, splashing each other in the waves, making sand castles and watching the ferry boats cross The Solent.

It was a very sleepy but happy boy that said, "Good-night Granma Phil," as I tucked him up in bed.

I still had my ride in the evening, but I too was glad when the time came for bed.

There was one good thing about riding someone else's horse, no mucking out, no grooming, just a friendly pat on the neck, a stroke or two and a tid-bit of sugar.

On a further occasion I was invited to the home of my rescuer, the caretaker, his home was in the village of Beaulie, near the stately home of Beaulie Manor, where there was housed some of the finest antique cars in the world.

It was a shame I never had time to visit this Manor, although it was thrown open to the public on certain days, but not being mechanically minded I wasn't too upset. Anyway, I came to ride horses not gaze at automobiles....

And in that week I must have rode at least six different horses, from liver-chestnut's to grey's, a strawberry-roan and a sixteen-hand black gelding with large feet and a stubborn mouth.

I was quite chuffed on the whole as not once was I unseated.

I had a wonderful time and made many friends, and my hostess told me I would be welcome to stay any time.

I never told her then — that it was to be my last riding holiday in England, as my husband had planned that we would be spending our retiring years on the other side of the ocean, in Canada. His homeland, and that coming October not only would we be visiting family and friends, but I would be applying for my immigration papers while we were there.

How would I tell my family? But I think they had already guessed, and another blow was to follow.

The horses would have to go.

# Chapter Twenty-Four

# THE LAST GOOD-BYES

People talk freely about starting life anew, talk's cheap, but when it comes to the final crunch, it's a serious business.

In my case there were five children to leave behind, grown-ups that was true, but still children to me.

Geoffrey had gone on ahead of us, his new life as fate had planned was with a young Canadian girl he had met six months previous. Thus history was repeating itself with an unusual twist. So at least one of our flock had left us without a qualm. When we decided to leave the others, that didn't go down too well.

"You can always follow us there," we said.

Little thinking that within the next two year's one of them would. Young Ray.

A few years later my daughter and her family, and the following year, my son Laurence and his little brood.

Our lives had altered considerably during the later years. There was no family residing at home. Joan and Margaret had moved from the county, and our friends over the years, Vic and June were set to move to Ongar Village just a short time after we departed from the English shore.

The grazing land behind the house and the surrounding pasture had turned into a bricks and mortar jungle, and our dear friends the Metsons, Hilda and George were retiring from farming.

Their sons still intended to farm the land at Doddinghurst, but the land was to be sold to The Essex Agricultural College.

I was wondering how they would cope with the ever-increasing number of trespassers who had started to invade the fields.

Time and time again the fences were broken, wires cut, and even the padlocks on the gates were often shot off by roaming vandals. Twice in one week, someone had tried to steal the horses.

It was all getting too difficult for just Bertie and myself to cope. So, perhaps it was just as well that on my last visit to Canada in the late October, I made my final decision to immigrate, and, as much as I would miss my four-legged friends they would have to go.

However, we did ride Foxy and Melody right up to the last weekend before they were sold. My friend Joan introduced us to a farmer friend from the tiny village of Ugly, he was keen on Foxy, we agreed upon a price which included the saddle and bridle too. Melody, Joan kept for awhile, I always knew she was very fond of her and one Saturday morning at the beginning of May, Joan and Angie came to collect them.

I never went to the field with Bertie to see them go, coward that I was, I left him to see to it all. He was choked when he came back and so was I, whenever I went into the garage and saw the empty spaces where the saddles sometimes used to hang and the bare hooks along the wall bereft of bridles.

We sold the house, but only after much aggravation, when hordes of strange people would flock to the door and mill around all over the house, some with no intention of buying as they made their stupid offers that they knew we would refuse.

Most of our worldly possessions, we either sold or gave away, but there were some things that I just couldn't part with.

My Jodhpurs, for instance, hat, boots and spurs, those things I have to this very day.

After most of our things had gone and the house had been sold subject to contract, I still had something to worry about. It was my Canadian Visa, it still hadn't made its appearance.

What was I to do? I asked myself. We'd already sold the shot-guns.

Eventually, everything in order, we were ready to leave, the flight was scheduled for the end of May, which gave us a few days grace to stay with my daughter for the last weekend.

We had made so many friends over the years, so there were so many good-bye parties to go to and we also had another daughter-in-law to say farewell to, another Mrs. Holden to swell the ranks. Her name was Nicola, Carl's new wife and within the next three years there were also two more grandchildren, I had run out of fingers to count. Bertie had made his mark in England even if he wasn't going to live there anymore.

We flew away at the end of May, the family came to the airport to wave us good-bye. I cried all the way across the ocean as I recalled the faces of my family and friends and my beloved horses, and I made a promise to return for a holiday to see most of them again.

I did, a few years later ....

And as I turned from the field-gate without a backward glance to tread the well-ridden path towards the road and the last gate I thought I heard them calling me.

The ghostly whinnies of a bygone day.

THE END.

# EPILOGUE

Frosty lived to a ripe old age, winning many more cups and ribbons. Cobber died a year after we left England, and Lady Jane died after giving birth to her first foal.

My youngest son was the first to join us in Canada, but he died two years after at the age of twenty-five.

My daughter joined us with her husband and her three daughters four years later, but fate played a cruel trick on them when Brian, after waiting so long to join us, died within the first two weeks.

I have my grandchildren here with me now as well as my son Laurence and his family.

We have no Marion Mould's or Harvey Smith's as yet.

Who knows, maybe time and fate will tell.

I have my memories and how wonderful they are even though I shall never ride again ......